Praise for

"Finally, a book about manifesting everyone Kris Ferraro takes the mystery out of manifesting, making this powerful practice accessible to all. Packed with tips, tools, inspirational quotes, and hands-on exercises, this will be one book you are going to want to keep around. If you are wondering how to create a life of happiness and prosperity, look no further."
—Sherianna Boyle, author of
Emotional Detox Now

"*Manifesting* is a practical, essential guide for anyone who wants to turn their dreams into reality. Kris Ferraro has every detail covered: why we need to manifest, potential obstacles and how to overcome them, tools we can use to make manifestation easier, how to tailor the process to your individual needs, and much more. This empowering book is truly a must-read."
—Katie Beecher, MS, LPC, medical intuitive and
licensed counselor, and author of *Heal from Within:*
A Guidebook for Intuitive Wellness

"I was hooked the moment I read the first sentence of Kris Ferraro's book. Instead of glossing over the hard stuff and fluffing up her wins, Ferraro invites us into her story with a broken heart. Over the past three decades, I've read many classics on manifesting and the law of attraction. I often noticed there was one thing that fell short for me. I'd read each basic formula that combined affirmation of the unlimited abundance of the Universe, cultivation of gratitude, and a saccharine insistence on positivity. Yet it always felt like something was missing. These books withheld all the messy, miserable pitfalls which inevitably stop us in our tracks. Truth about the struggle is the thing that so many self-help and spiritual development books lack. Not this book though. Ferraro brings her raw, real, authentic self to this wonderful guide. She offers amazing tools, while also sharing her unvarnished truth. I'm so thankful for her willingness to teach about manifestation in a way that includes the hard, sticky, snot-covered reality of human life. It became a lot easier to keep going when I grasped that creating a life of our dreams doesn't always happen effortlessly and easily. This book is the perfect combination of straightforward, doable actions, inspiring pep-talk, and emotional validation. In the same way that Ferraro's book *Energy Healing* has something for the newbie and the seasoned energy practitioner, this book has gems for anyone hoping to up their manifesting game. Even as a seasoned practitioner of metaphysics and energy healing, I found tips, tools, perspective, and encouragement. I have no doubt this will be another treasured volume in my library for many years to come."

—Jennifer Elizabeth Moore, master trainer for EFT International, and author of *Empathic Mastery: A 5-Step System to Go from Emotional Hot Mess to Thriving Success*

"Kris Ferraro offers recipe after recipe for shifting and creating a life you love. And she's a smart, hip, well-versed guide that talks to you like your best friend. Grab this playbook again and again—because there's just so much packed into this quick, juicy read."

—Tama Kieves, USA featured visionary career coach, and bestselling author of *Inspired & Unstoppable: Wildly Succeeding in Your Life's Work!*

Manifesting

Also by Kris Ferraro

*Energy Healing: Simple and Effective
Practices to Become Your Own Healer*

*Ultimate Energy: Using Your Natural
Energies to Balance Body, Mind, and
Spirit* (with Tori Hartman and Eliza Swann)

Manifesting

**THE PRACTICAL, SIMPLE GUIDE TO
CREATING THE LIFE YOU WANT**

Kris Ferraro

ST. MARTIN'S
ESSENTIALS
NEW YORK

First published in the United States by St. Martin's Essentials, an imprint of St. Martin's Publishing Group

Designed by Ralph Fowler

www.stmartins.com

Library of Congress Cataloging-in-Publication Data

Names: Ferraro, Kris, author.
Title: Manifesting : the practical, simple guide to creating the life you want / Kris Ferraro.
Description: First edition. | New York : St. Martin's Essentials, 2021. | Includes index. | Identifiers: LCCN 2021008161 | ISBN 9781250769558 (trade paperback) | ISBN 9781250769541 (ebook)
Subjects: LCSH: Success. | Self-actualization (Psychology) | Self-realization. | Spirituality.
Classification: LCC BJ1611.2 .F465 2021 | DDC 158.1—dc23
LC record available at https://lccn.loc.gov/2021008161

Our books may be purchased in bulk for promotional, educational, or business use. Please contact your local bookseller or the Macmillan Corporate and Premium Sales Department at 1-800-221-7945, extension 5442, or by email at MacmillanSpecialMarkets@macmillan.com.

First Edition: 2021

10 9 8 7 6 5 4 3 2

For trailblazing misfits, modern mystics, miracle midwives, bold-and-shy dreamers, and out-of-the-box believers everywhere

This is for you

Contents

PART TWO
The 9 Powerful Manifesting Alchemy Practices

PART FOUR

Bringing Manifesting Alchemy into the World

Introduction

TO MANIFESTING AND ALCHEMY

About Me

I had arrived in Denver with a broken heart. Some months before, a seemingly chance encounter had brought me into a full-on soul-to-soul connection with a kindred spirit. That sense of suddenly being at home in another's presence. Of having known each other before. It had surprised and delighted me. In an instant, I saw many potential possibilities for a future "us." It's something us manifestors are known for. We believe truly anything is possible and often visualize what we want. But in the time since, it became increasingly clear that this yummy possibility would not come to fruition after all. Bereft, I had woken from my fog and realized I wasn't going to get what I wanted here. Not with this guy anyway. Just in time for a scheduled cross-country conference, I carried my heavyhearted disappointment onto the plane, along with my overloaded suitcase.

> You belong in the life of your dreams. And you don't belong anywhere else.
>
> —Tama Kieves

It might seem like an odd or bold choice to start a book on manifestation by fully admitting a recent failure. A time I was way off. Featuring none other than "the one that got away." You'd be absolutely right to think that. And this wouldn't be the first time the words *odd* or *bold* would be used to describe me and my choices.

I mean, after all, shouldn't I be a glowing example of the perfect life? Every dream realized, every wish fulfilled, with nothing left to do but sit on a beach, drinking mai tais and counting my money while Mr. Right massages my feet?

———————

Well, dear readers / future manifestors / dream weavers, I have a much, much more interesting journey to share.

In the twenty-three years since I started actively creating what I wanted, my life has changed so dramatically, I can hardly recognize myself. I am happier, healthier, more prosperous, and more creative, and I love myself more than I ever knew was possible. And along the way, I've also encountered every possible pitfall, wrong turn, and pure delusion that can greet you on this journey. The ego snafus. The things I created I wish I hadn't. The old stories and beliefs that got in the way. And I'm going to share it all, along with steps for recognizing and healing these missteps. We all have them. The creative process is fraught with what can feel like failures. But what's fascinating is the "mistakes" end up being an essential part of uncovering your best life.

Because the last thing the world needs is a self-help book that ultimately makes people feel bad about themselves. Not happening. Not on my watch!

So back in Denver, I'd finished off the second day of the conference and had an hour free before I met a group for dinner. My hotel room had a comfy round love seat with an ottoman and velour pillows. I curled up there with a blanket and my laptop, my eyes taking turns between a Netflix stand-up comedy special and the gentle snow blowing past the window. It had been an unusually warm winter in my home state of New Jersey, and I had been craving just this, snow.

I glanced at my phone to check the time: 4:30 p.m. Thirty minutes until dinner.

It seemed like such a mundane act. Checking the time. Something I can do five hundred times a day. Wasn't exactly what one would expect for entrance into a supernatural experience. There were no drums beating, no chanting, no scent of incense in the air. No deities descended into the room, trumpets blaring, sharing profound news. But that's exactly what it ended up being.

In my mind, I was transported back in time to ten years before. I was sitting in my office where I was a counselor in a social service agency. At that point, I had been there for thirteen years, which was already five years too long. What had once been a dream job had turned into a nightmare. I had grown and evolved past what was conceivable in this setting. My approach to being in service to others had shifted, and I felt stifled, frustrated, and bored. There was no room for me to bring to the job what I was most passionate about. Outside of the office, I was learning everything I could on manifestation, energy, and healing. Reading books, meditating, praying, visualizing, tapping, balancing. All that ended at my office door.

In the meantime, the job description, CEO, funding, and the company itself had changed, none for the better. But within that ever-widening gap between who I was becoming and where I remained was that darn security with all its plain-Jane seduction. Paid vacation and holidays. Good benefits. And a guaranteed source of income, every two weeks, right on time. How could I possibly leave? I looked up at the clock: 4:30 p.m. Thirty more minutes. Thirty interminable minutes. Every day had become in some ways the same day, and my adventurous spirit was dying. I was either counting down the minutes to freedom or the days until a holiday or a vacation. I spent each lunch hour numbing out to what I affectionately called "online travel porn," watching other people visit exotic countries, hike through jungles, share gourmet meals with new friends, essentially living the kind of life I wanted to live. And here I was, staring at the clock, waiting for 5:00 p.m. and the temporary freedom on the other side of it.

Then in an instant, I snapped back into the present day. My mind, heart, and body became flooded with gratitude and love. Here I was, 4:30 on a Tuesday, curled up in a beautiful room, in a lively city I had never been to and always wanted to visit, laughing and savoring the sweetness of it all. Here I was, in a hotel filled with loving, kind, fellow manifestors, spending my day listening to heart-opening live music and inspirational talks, my travel paid for. On an ordinary Tuesday! Can you believe it? Here I was, counting down the minutes to join sweet friends for a farm-to-table dinner, where we would share deep appreciation for one another in a way that brought tears to my eyes. One would mention a particularly valuable quality he felt I brought to our team's efforts, and I was awakened by it. Here, I learned something new about myself. Here I was, in a career I cherished, helping others in the ways I know truly work and sharing the good news of that to anyone who would listen. Speaking, traveling, teaching, and sharing healing on stages, on podcasts, and in interviews. Here I was, living the life I had always wanted to live. This was it. I was and am here.

If I had a selfie stick and captured this, I have to tell you, the scene would not have appeared Instagram-worthy. No beach, no Mr. Right, no size 6, and honestly, the lighting in that room was just terrible. There wasn't even a fan to give me that sexy blowing-hair look. And remember, there were no mystical lights or signs. But I was exactly where I had always wanted to be. No time clock to punch. No waiting for the interminable minutes to tick by, rescuing me from my miserable reality. No numbing out to images of others' lives.

My temporary heartache had had me distracted, focusing my mind and energy on the one thing in my life that wasn't working (yet). Perhaps that sounds familiar. Have you ever had a paper cut? Those painful little suckers will force your attention on lockdown. Here 99.9999 percent of your body is just fine, and you keep thinking about that paper cut. *Why doesn't the company just go paperless already? And this wouldn't have happened if they had lotion in the restrooms, and I really should be drinking more water or my skin wouldn't be this dry, and how come nobody seems to be able to create a softer paper? And man, this really hurts! And . . . and . . . and . . .* You could stay trapped in that loop forever!

A divine intervention generously cut through my despair and reminded me of what I had lost sight of. I have created—and will continue creating—the life I've always wanted. And I've done that using the very principles, practices, and skills I am sharing here. All in a no-nonsense, no-BS, no-squeaky-shiny-image kind of way.

> To be normal is the ideal aim of the unsuccessful.
>
> —Carl Jung

Becoming a manifestor meant becoming more of my true self, with all my edges, weirdness, and ultra-realness coming into hyper-focus. I'll leave the Kardashians and the rest of the influencers to their soul purposes. They know what they're doing. Mine looks different, and so does yours.

Yes. You *can* create the beach, the money, a tight butt, and a beautiful love relationship. Or anything else you want as well.

Not overnight. (Although some manifestations happen quite quickly. Growth is a process. And you will be growing.)

Not all at once. (There's always something to work on.)

And your ideal life may indeed look insta-picture-perfect. Or it may look like ordinary on steroids. Or it may seem to the outside world like a fun house mirror strapped to roller skates on a Ferris wheel, but it will make sense to you.

It just might look like something you could never have expected at all.

What I can guarantee is that adventure awaits.

You were born with a sacred mission.

We all know this intuitively. We are most in touch with this knowing when we've lost sight of it. We're feeling unsatisfied and unfulfilled. We realize one, five, or forty years have passed and we still haven't (fill in the blank) _____ (gone to China, written that book, paid off the debt, learned to sail). Within that discontent is your ticket out of it.

Allow it to move you forward.

To take a chance.

To take a risk that you are more than what you think you are.

And that you're capable of more than you know right now.

And that maybe, just maybe, you can have more than you've dreamed possible.

And that there is a power in the Universe supporting you every single step of the way.

Our goals realized bring the amenities of life. The bonuses, the extras, the gifts. The empty hotel hot tub. The delivery of fragrant flowers. Room service at the perfect time. They come from saying yes to your mission to be who you came to this planet to be. But what you let go of on the path to the goals: the misguided ideas about yourself, the painful memories, and ill-fitting cultural conditioning, that's the good stuff. You get it. You really get it. You're worthy of more. And you, with all the things you don't like about yourself, will realize you are unconditionally loved and supported by a Power Greater Than Yourself. Exactly as you are right now. And I'm not just referring to the metaphorical "you" authors use. I'm actually talking about *you*. Do you know how I know that? How I can say that when we've likely never met? Because we all are. Those inner longings, to love and be loved, to express, to create, to achieve, to wake up, and feel better already are calling you

> There is no greater thing you can do with your life and your work than follow your passions in a way that serves the world and you.
>
> —**Sir Richard Branson**

forward into more. May this book be a friendly companion and guide to support that process.

Manifesting *Is* Alchemy: Turn the Lead of Your Life into Gold

There is a reason why you've chosen to read this book. Everything, every choice, has a reason.

There's something or somethings that you feel you're missing. Or you've been stuck and nothing is moving forward. Or there's a still, small voice inside that whispers, *There's more to life than this. There's got to be.*

Maybe you've been struggling financially. Perhaps this struggle feels eternal, like it's always been there, or possibly recent events have turned your once solid financial world upside down.

> There is nothing more important than developing your imagination to transform your life from the inside world of your thoughts and feelings to the outside world of your results and manifestations.
>
> **—Neville Goddard**

What about love? Do you have a heart longing to be ensconced in the arms of a happy partnership? Have other attempts at true love simply missed the mark?

Or your health and vitality are lagging and the aging process is unmercifully speeding up. There's only so many supplements a person can take.

And then there's career and accomplishment. Do you grow numb the second you get to the office? For once, can you just get into a line of work where you thrive already?

Normally, we approach these changes from the outside, trying to make different choices "out there" to create a change of state "in here."

You get a Costco membership and cancel cable to save money, hoping that will give you a greater sense of security. Or you download the latest dating app. Maybe this pool of people will connect you to the One. You find an exercise video on YouTube and get cracking on improving your health. Or hire a career counselor to offer direction.

In and of themselves, these could be all worthwhile choices. But we are going to leave the action steps for later.

First, we start with creating change from the inside out.

You're entering a journey. A journey where you will consciously create what you want to do, be, and have.

You're soon to become an alchemist!

That's what the act of manifesting is all about. The alchemists of old spent lifetimes on the pursuit of turning the material of lead into gold. They didn't hop on a horse or camel or wander aimlessly in the forest or desert looking for gold. They took what they had and transformed it.

> Everything that exists is in a manner the seed of that which will be.
>
> **—Marcus Aurelius**

And once you've embraced the alchemical principles and practices, you'll realize that *you* are a powerful creator. And it didn't take a lifetime to become one!

Let's get started!

Why Take a Chance on Manifesting?

I'm asking you to take a giant leap of faith here.

I'm asking you to believe that you're capable of having, being, and doing more. And I'm asking you at the same time to love yourself and your life right now as they are. I'm asking you to open to what for me was a radical concept: that creating a succulent and satisfying life can be fun, simple, and exciting. I know full well you will come face-to-face with a few limiting beliefs, old memories, and people to forgive. And that isn't the fun part. But on the other side of letting the past go is the buoyancy we all crave. To flow with the rhythms of life instead of sinking. And I don't approach any of this lightly.

> We are far larger, more daring, and more creative than we imagine.
>
> **—Julia Cameron**

Settling

Our deepest longings are vulnerable parts of ourselves. Maybe when you were growing up, your needs and desires weren't met, or were ignored or even shunned. Maybe you experienced a disappointment with a heartbreak or other loss. Those longings got buried under settling. Settling for what is, what's easy, what's around. But those desires are still within you, awaiting your attention.

Here's what I've learned about settling. As a former safe player, settling was always appealing to me. "Just accept what is, Kris. This _____ (job, love, opportunity) may not be what you really wanted. But at least it's _____ (here now, available, being offered). Be grateful already! Who are you to expect more?" And then a most unsettling thing would happen each time I settled. The yeses, the checked boxes, the good parts about what I had settled for would change. The seemingly loyal but selfish boyfriend mocked me to a mutual friend. The job's great benefits became less great, then not so good, then nonexistent. I would observe helplessly as what met a few of my needs was slowly eroded.

You always end up settling for less than what you originally planned for.

I'm going to say this: Take a chance on more. Take a chance that there is a benevolent force for good in the Universe and you can work with it. Take the risk! You are worth it.

And if you're still asking why you should bother, here are points to consider.

The Status Quo Is Overrated

The status quo is the current nature of existing states of your life. As it is, right now. You can be grateful for all that you have now, and I encourage this. It doesn't mean you can't also desire more. Status quo = the same. The same = safe. Safe = boring. Safe = unfulfilling. Safe = potential passing you by. Safe = believing you don't deserve more. No matter who you are, no matter what life looks like for you, I'm happy to share that there is more available.

Every single person who ever advanced civilization forward, whether that was in areas of entertainment, arts, politics, social justice, science, technology, economics, philosophy, agriculture, and more, was someone who decided there could be another way. There could be a better way. You can be that kind of person as well. Do you want to advance the very nature of life? Or accept what's unconsciously been created so far? You have that chance right now.

> To live is the rarest thing in the world. Most people just exist.
> —Oscar Wilde

Being Open Feels Better Than Being Closed

This says it all. Being closed is like living inside of a cage. Each time you're presented with a new possibility, you run headfirst into the bars. Ouch! Openness feels light, soft, and free. And don't we all want to feel that? Even when what's possible feels outside your current comfort zone, the other side of fear is excitement. That excitement can carry you forward to big ideas. Those big ideas then become big manifestations.

Changing Yourself Creates Change for Others

As you change, as your life changes, your very essence or energy field changes into one of potent potentiality. Without saying a word, you become a living embodiment of prosperity, health, vitality, love. And you bring yourself wherever you go. This creates shifts in the collective consciousness. Want to change the world? Changing yourself creates change in the field, affecting everyone. When enough people live from this place,

> Dwell in possibility.
> **—Emily Dickinson**

radical positive change will occur across the globe. Closer to home, the relationships with the people in your immediate circle begin to shift. Empowered people empower others. Changed people know change isn't only possible, it's actually quite doable. And transformed people know how to transform life as we know it, creating good for everyone else, not just themselves.

As Long as You're Living, You Might as Well Be Growing

Actually, your soul is here to grow. And even attempting to keep anything the same won't work. The Universe is always in a state of expansion. Have you ever watched an old movie, like say from the '50s? I like to do this every now and again because it's an example of the prevailing technology, beliefs, culture, and yes, consciousness of the time. In 1998, when director Gus Van Sant decided to create a shot-by-shot remake of the classic Hitchcock film *Psycho,* I knew it wouldn't work. Life had changed dramatically since the original was released. The results were a stiff, stilted, and not-scary facsimile. It tried to re-create a product of that time and space. Going backward never produces anything meaningful. It moves against the forward flow of energy. So if you're here to grow, then why not grow consciously? If you don't, you may be faced with situations where growth feels forced upon you. You are always working with Universal laws, whether you want to or not. Choosing to work *with* them creates a supportive collaboration.

Yes, You Can Get More "Stuff," and That Feels Good!

This is likely why you're here, why you picked up this book. There are things you want that you don't now have. A new computer. Money for a vacation. A job you love. A love you'd love. Attracting these items into your life is a very good thing. How happy you are is the only success quotient there is. A new computer will make almost every project in your life easier. A vacation offers relaxation, fun, a much-needed break, which boosts health and mood. You spend many hours each week at your job. How joyous will that feel when your vocation is an ideal fit? A love helps you experience the Universe's love in human form. Everything you want is because of how it will make you feel. Having what you want feels good. People who feel good often do good.

Trust in the Universe

I haven't met a person whose life didn't contain some level of disappointment. When that happens, we can lack trust in life and ourselves. Manifesting helps develop a rock-solid trust. Trust in yourself to create a better, more enjoyable, more meaningful life. Then you develop trust in the Higher Power of Your Own Understanding. To learn that there is this source of all that is or could ever be, and it's here for you, listening and providing for you . . . That. Changes. Everything.

> Without leaps of imagination, or dreaming, we lose the excitement of possibilities. Dreaming, after all, is a form of planning.
>
> —Gloria Steinem

I remember it like it was yesterday. I was twenty-seven years old and taking a workshop to change unconscious beliefs. We learned and worked with affirmations, visualizations, and self-hypnosis. Even though I had been on a spiritual journey since I was a young child, my life at this point was not working well for me; I was currently unemployed, and I had grown cynical. Well, cynical and even more desperate.

The desperation overrode my pessimism long enough to find practices to change my life. In this workshop, while doing a guided visualization, I became aware of this feeling in my chest. It was both completely new to me and somehow entirely familiar. This tender, sweet, encompassing warmth spread throughout my body, bringing a profound realization. I began to cry. I knew. I was loved. Me? *Me.* I couldn't believe it. Me with all my insecurities, mistakes, and fears. Me for whom nothing ever seemed to work out. Me who felt like the forever oddball, the black sheep, the one least likely to succeed. An instantaneous shift happened that changed me forever. Brain cells were reorganized. Everything up until that moment stopped. I knew. The Universe was real. Like really real. It was a true revelation. An odd confession, I realize, from a person who was grasping at any possible spiritual solution available. But until then, the Universe was just a concept. A set of ideas. A mental construct based on all I had been exposed to and then explored. Those explorations were based on other people's experiences of a Higher Power, not my own. This force was something I hoped existed, but in all honesty, I didn't know that it did. I hadn't even admitted that to myself. Until that moment in time.

> The more you believe it, the more it starts to become real for you. This is why it is so very important to believe in positive things, rather than negative things. Whatever you believe, you will find that you are correct. The universe has a way of presenting to you exactly what you believe. If you think life is great, you are correct. If you think life is tough, you will be proved correct too.
>
> **—Anita Moorjani**

And I have witnessed so often in the lives of many how the difference between sickness and health, addiction and sobriety, lack and abundance, is exactly this. That inner realization, revelation, spiritual truth that each of us is indeed loved. We are never alone.

Finding this, in your own time and way, is worth the time, the energy, and yes, the risks. On your manifesting journey, it begins with developing that highly personal communication with a force that responds. You work with the language of words, feelings, mental images, and actions; you are communicating who you are and what you want. Asking for guidance, reading signs, and receiving intuitive information is how the Universe speaks back. From this, you develop the most important relationship you can ever have. It's both the one with your truest self and the Higher Power of All That Is. You will uncover that they are one in the same.

Can You Create What You Desire?

Everything that exists was once just an idea. The roads you drive on. The dwelling in which you live. That movie from last night. The evolution of species are ideas of adaptation born within. This very book started as an idea that eventually was then given to me to create. The ideas of this book's inception met my ideas. These ideas coupled up with my experience, expertise, and wisdom. They met all that I had learned from so many others. Then they met action, the very writing and editing. What's written will go to people. And where once there was nothing, now there is this hopeful tome.

> Just remember life is all an illusion . . . it's your creation and you can dismantle it and re-create at will.
> —Nanette Mathews

Everything visible was once invisible. The creative process is the story of life, every aspect of life. Single-cell organisms eventually become the complexity that is us. Within us all are the seeds of our beginnings, the promise of those single cells. Within you are seeds of ideas awaiting to burst open with their potential. They already have their perfectly encoded

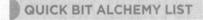
QUICK BIT ALCHEMY LIST

5 Powerful Ways to Start Your Day

1. **Wake up your energy.** Rub under both sides of your collarbone on the upper chest, breathing in through the nose and out through the mouth, for about two minutes.

2. **Jump up and down with your hands high in the air, smiling, and exclaiming, "Yes, yes, yes!"**

3. **Drink warm water with fresh lemon juice while affirming your health and vitality. Livers need decluttering too.**

4. **Sing along to inspirational music.**

5. **Read passages from sacred or motivational sources.**

blueprints within them. They just need to be planted in fertile soil and given water and sun. This book will help you get clear about the seeds of your ideas and desires. Then give you attitudes, principles, and practices to create nourishing conditions in which they come to life.

First I must ask: What's believable to you?

I ask myself this all the time. For example, do I believe a ninety-year-old woman can become an astronaut? I honestly don't. But why is that? Is it based on dated ideas I have about aging, gender, or even NASA? Right now, there are women in their nineties who are writing novels, leading businesses, teaching yoga, and performing in films. Why can't they go to space?

Being a manifestor means stretching beyond what you have believed is possible for yourself. And that can mean changing what you believe is possible, period.

My astronaut belief above won't garner my time and attention in changing it. Because I'm not a ninety-year-old woman who wants to go to space. But there are plenty of others I have changed because they affected my ability to create what I want.

Life forms to our beliefs about it.

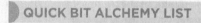

QUICK BIT ALCHEMY LIST

21 Amazing Manifestors Who Inspire Me

1. Bruce Springsteen
2. Catherine Ponder
3. The Dalai Lama
4. Danielle LaPorte
5. David Bowie
6. Deepak Chopra
7. Gary Craig
8. Gregg Braden
9. Henry David Thoreau
10. Saint Hildegard of Bingen
11. Dr. Joe Dispenza
12. Kate Sessions
13. Oprah Winfrey
14. Marianne Williamson
15. Myrtle and Charles Fillmore
16. Napoleon Hill
17. Nikola Tesla
18. Ralph Waldo Emerson
19. Saint Padre Pio
20. Salvador Dalí
21. Wayne Dyer

We Are Here to Grow

Why are we here?

This is a question I don't believe everyone asks themselves, not once in an entire lifetime. There are people who are content to be born, grow up, get a job, have a family, and retire without ever asking, "Why me? Why was I born? What am I doing here?" That's a perfectly fine way to make a go of life. There are times I still wish I had been one of those people. Like when I'm hectic with a deadline looming and I look over at my napping cat Ling. Forever Zen, she opens her sleepy eyes, yawns, glances my way, and the look is always the same, "What's wrong *now*?" She doesn't get it. The existential crises, the tightrope walks over rocky terrain. She lives in acceptance and rhythm. All is right in her world, every single day. The animals have it all figured out. Me, not so much. I chide myself, "Why, oh, why can't this be me? I could drop out of life right now and go scrub floors in an ashram!" The voice of my overwhelm always offers solutions that include, one, leaving my entire life behind for, two, some kind of obedient spiritual job in the middle of nowhere. Pulling potatoes in a monastery garden. Being chief dishwasher in a convent. And I detest doing dishes! Can you imagine how desperate I would feel to consider such a thing? And if I shared those ideas with anyone who knows me, I'd be confronted with a mixture of shock and hilarity. Because I will never be a simple-life kind of gal. I'd last mere minutes before tearing off my robes, throwing them in the wood-burning stove, and yelling, "I'm out of here!" while stomping out in those hideously functional boots. This would likely occur during a time of silence. Thankfully, I wasn't born to adopt anyone else's idea of who I am and what an ideal spiritual life looks like. And you weren't either. Manifesting at its best is becoming more and more of yourself, even in ways that can astonish you.

When I'm not seeking escape, I'm positively thrilled my calling has been to unleash my inner Conscious Cocreator, a Miracle Receiver, and Mischievous Manifestor. After all, I was born ruminating on the big questions. As a young child, I remember seeing a copy of *National Geographic*. It contained spectacular photos of the Milky Way. I remember thinking, *Who are we and why are we here?* Feel a bit of compassion for my poor parents.

> We must be willing to let go of the life we planned so as to have the life that is waiting for us.
>
> —Joseph Campbell

They didn't quite know what to do with me. Thank God I received a fervent curiosity for finding answers to go along with those deep questions. On the power days, the bold and beautiful days, when everything is flowing my way, I sneer, "Guess what, status quo? You can bite me! I didn't come here to follow the crowd. I'm advancing civilization forward. And you're welcome!"

I don't believe we are just clumps of clustered cells with a heartbeat. I know with certainty we are not the blabbering nonsense of our monkey minds. That's a relief! There were times I thought I was my crippling anxiety and fears. Got to watch out for those. They're very convincing. But within me, there has always been a deeper knowing. I didn't learn it from my parents, school, or church. It's always just been there, a soft assurance, a whisper of more. Imagine a compass, a lighthouse, a movable manifesto written in poetry and song, all calling me forward, beckoning me to look beyond what I see with my eyes. It's been there all along.

When I ask why I'm here, at this time, at this place, in a body, doing what I do, the best answers are obvious. And they start with more specific questions.

What gives me joy? (Lifelong learning, creative projects realized, dancing.) What unleashes a zeal and passion within me for living? (Healing, belief in possibilities, travel.) What gets me up in the morning? (My vocation, desire to help, time with people I love.)

Conversely, when I'm dragging myself out of bed, what's the problem? (Exhaustion, overscheduling, feeling misunderstood.) What qualities in others make me light up? (Openness, depth, trustworthiness.) When do I experience something greater than myself? (In prayer, nature, and the beauty of art, music, and design.)

Because that's what makes life juicy and satisfying for me. Love. Purpose. Service. Expansion. Humor. Connection. Empowerment. Peace. Beauty. These qualities may be similar for you, and at the same time, your examples may appear completely unique. Your vocation or the one you're seeking to create will reflect your soul's purpose, not mine. Your awe-inspiring nature experiences may be near the ocean while mine are in the mountains. And nature is our value. If I could poll a million people with these same questions, I can guarantee the answers would fall in the categories above. This would be regardless of country, culture, beliefs, or religion. Because they are Universal truths, inherent within all life. We can never be separated from them. And none of these qualities can be identified in a blood test. Your doctor will never say, "I'm sorry, but your tests indicate you are dangerously low on joy." And quite frankly, I'd welcome a day when doctors can share spiritual concerns such as this. Because as I shared, we are more than just a clump of cells. And what can bring us to the doctor's office—or bankruptcy court, for that matter—can have a great deal to do with spiritual deficits. And if those deficits aren't addressed by your doctor or lawyer, their solutions for you may be temporary. Spiritual principles and practices are the perfect accompaniment to everything you're doing to heal and feel and live better. And until your doctor and lawyer are trained on these matters, it's time for you to step up and be your own spiritual teacher. You can become so effective at manifesting a happy, healthy life, you may not need them so much anymore anyway!

> What is now proved was once only imagined.
>
> —William Blake

Manifesting Reflection Questions on Purpose

1. Why do you believe you are here?

2. What gives you joy?

3. You wake up one day filled with excitement. You can't wait for this day to begin! What's happening?

4. What qualities make the people in your life special to you?

5. What gives all life meaning?

6. What gives your life meaning?

7. How would you feel if your life had more meaning now?

8. Describe the experience that left you the most inspired.

9. List three people you consider to be heroes. These can be entertainers, celebrities, politicians, philanthropists, or historical figures. Under each, describe why they are heroes to you. What qualities did or do they possess?

Within these answers, you've collected valuable information that will help you craft a vision for a more inspired, meaningful life. As you continue reading, exploring, and practicing the exercises that follow, keep this information in mind. Think of it as "the big picture" and you're filling it in with the weather, terrain, people, and objects you'd like to be in it.

How "It" Works and What to Call "It"

There is a force of creation. And you can use it.

You're already using it. You can't shut it off. You can't shut it down.

This force created you. Like a hologram, the smallest piece contains the integrity of the whole. You are that piece.

You have used it to create every facet of your life.

It is the energy that creates all of life. Every single bit of it. Everything that has ever taken form since the dawn of existence and everything that could ever be made real. And if there was anything before the start of existence, it was there as well. It likely simply always just was. It is the invisible substance that is formless. It is the mold. It is the creation. It is every step of the evolution of the creation.

Single-cell organisms. The bacteria lining intestines. A tiny shard of broken clear glass in an empty parking lot. A speck of pollen falling from a flower petal. The steel, glass, and blueprint of the Empire State Building. And everything and everyone inside it. Each sheet of paper. Every desk chair. The smallest fiber from a carpet, swirling unnoticed in the air. The same force that comprises the rings around Saturn. A power so varied it has diversified into over sixty thousand species of trees.

Every idea ever conceived. Ones that became visible. And ones that never did.

The particles of light, vibration, and sound that take all form.

> Inquire within, rather than without, asking: What part of my Self do I wish to experience now? What aspects of being do I choose to call forth? For all of life exists as a tool of your own creation, and all of its events merely present themselves as opportunities for you to decide, and be, Who You Are.
>
> **—Neale Donald Walsch**

And it just keeps creating. That's what it does.

This force is what quantum physicists call the Field and what theologians call God. You can call it whatever you want.

Just know this field, this force, this creative expression is everywhere, within you, and within all that's working and not working in your life. What you put into the force with your thoughts, feelings, and beliefs creates a prevailing consciousness that affects every aspect of your being. What you put in is what you get out.

I'm going to show you how to work with this force to create a life that makes you sing. There will be times that work looks like you're lassoing a bucking bronco. Other times you will kneel before it in trusting sweet surrender. You will be consciously working with the Creator of All That Is. An all-knowing force that knows you better than you know yourself.

When you show up to create knowing this, the work goes beyond just the stuff. Inner talents and strengths are unveiled within you that you had no idea were there. You develop deep faith, in yourself, in your worthiness, and your ability to be more of who you truly are. And you develop faith in that Higher Power to support, guide, and love you.

You realize you are never truly alone.

For this book, I'll use the term *Universe*. In my experience, this word seems the least triggering to the largest number of people. It's sciencey. It has no gender. And the connotation implies all-encompassing. It's also simply shorter than using Higher Power of Your Own Understanding. Yet, please know, Higher Power of Your Own Understanding (HPYOU) is exactly what I mean.

Where you see *Universe* in this book, feel free to mentally exchange that word for one that works for you. If you're coming into this work with already lovingly held beliefs on a Higher Power, use the term that helps you feel your connection to It. If that's God, that's beautiful. For some, the "G-word" has negative connotations. Maybe you were taught God is to be feared and that feels threatening to you. Then the word *God* is not your term. If you come from a religious background with a deity, then by all means, go with that. If you're generally spiritual, work with what you've used before. And if you're uncertain about all this and feeling flexible, experiment with what to call It. *Higher Self* is an excellent option for the more secularly minded. What helps you feel the love that is all around you? Spirit, Source, Life, Divine Love, Essence, Eternity, Great One, Lord, Father, Divine Mother. There are friends of mine who call it the *Unseen Therapist* and swear by this term. If you're feeling bold, come up with something on your own. "Make up a word for the Higher Power of My Own Understanding?" Yes, that's exactly what I'm saying. As your relationship with the HPYOU grows, the terminology you use becomes the doors. Doors to connection. Doors to bliss. Doors to blessings. Paint, adorn, and label that door so it's inviting to you.

I ended getting oddly traditional about all this. After test-driving an array of Higher Power Words from multiple disciplines over many years, I ended up back at *God*. It was very surprising to me. Here I was, a true spiritual rebel in every sense of the word, and I was not having a relationship with Deva or Brahman or the Flying Spaghetti Monster, but God? Seriously? But that's what worked for me. I learned the word itself didn't need to change. I had to let go of old conditioning and ideas I had about It, like the whole "old man in the sky" thing. The "has a gender" thing. Oh, and the punishing-condemnation thing too. And definitely the hating certain kinds of people myth. Yeah, none of that ever felt right and true, not even when I was a small child. Once my ideas about God came into resonance with what I intuitively understood as spiritual truths, I had what I needed. My doorway. And what I love about it is that word is just everywhere. On bumper stickers, billboards, journal covers, and in conversations. It does not matter if the bumper sticker owner and I are on the same theological page. For that moment, I feel a connection to the Higher Power of My Own Understanding—and to them, whoever they may be. If it helps me to love all people, well, then that's what God is supposed to be about.

I don't care what you call It. I just care that you call on It.

The Universe can feel highly impersonal. You focus on what you want. Create feelings that support that. Focus on the good. Good shows up. It's equally available for everyone. Not just available. It's already here whether you want it or not. It's inside you and all around you. You and everyone else on the planet. We all get to work with it to create what we want. When you know how to work it, it works.

But I don't recommend turning the Universe into your invisible vending machine.

Have you ever gotten a piece of clothing that was just perfect? Say, the ideal jacket that makes you feel gorgeous every time you wear it. You love it so much and will never want another! Fast-forward five years and you're using that same jacket to dry the muddy dog. Or perhaps you're a collector. You've been searching for years online for a limited print by artist Shepard Fairey. Finally, it's yours! Now framed and gracing a place of honor in your home, you soon walk past it without even a glance.

Things are good. Good to want, good to get. And yet the positive feelings they give us are temporary. After all, they're just things. Your desires are constantly evolving because energy is always evolving. Yes, use the information in this book to get what you want. Just don't stop there. Let it show you how to fall in love with yourself and life. And then love It back with all your heart.

> Life is ever giving of itself. We must receive, utilize and extend the gift. Success and prosperity are spiritual attributes belonging to all people.
>
> —Ernest Holmes

I invite you to bring deep reverence and respect to the Universe with this work.

Think of the person you love most in the world. Their photo may be the wallpaper on your phone, so you smile each time you pick it up. There are certainly photos of them in your home. You pass by an office building with a sign outside that contains their same name. You beam inside. Just a sighting of their name feels special. You mention their updates in conversations with other special people in your life. Maybe you pray for their well-being every day. They fill your conscious awareness with themselves. You give them valued importance in your mind and heart.

That's the kind of relationship I'd like you to have with the Universe. That love is perfect love. That love is eternal. That love is your love now.

How to Use This Book

This book contains theory, philosophy, stories, principles, tips, and practices. Wherever possible, I've outlined them in a linear format so you can find and return to needed sections with ease. Throughout, you will see references to visit other sections of the book, where these practices will be explained in greater detail. Because much like the creative process itself, the information here can be quite circular rather than a straight line.

> We build in thought the conditions that will later come into manifestation on the physical plane.
>
> —Emmet Fox

I would encourage you to read or at least skim the entire book from start to finish so you have an overall idea on all that it contains. Make a note of both that which inspires and that which challenges.

13 Motivating Quotes from Sacred Sources

1. **"We behold what we are, and we are what we behold."**
   —The Bhagavad Gita

2. **"Just as rain breaks through an ill-thatched house, so passion penetrates an undeveloped mind."** —The Dhammapada

3. **"Those who donate enthusiastically make constant efforts to increase their income so that they never find problems in making charity."** —The Veda

4. **"What you think, you become. What you feel, you attract. What you imagine, you create."** —The Buddha

5. **"Far beyond your intellect, far beyond your understanding, lies inexhaustible knowledge and wealth, strength and power, peace and joy. Do not use your intellect to find the answers for God and his manifestations. Everything is God."** —Vishnudevananda Saraswati

6. **"For I know the plans I have for you. Plans to prosper and not to harm you, plans to give you hope and a future."**
   —The Bible, Jeremiah 29:11

7. **"Give and it will be given to you. Good measure, pressed down, shaken together, running over, will be put into your lap. For with the measure you use it will be measured back to you."**
   —The Bible, Luke 6:38

8. **"You are altogether beautiful, my love; there is no flaw in you."**
   —The Bible, Song of Solomon 4:7

9. **"And let steadfastness have its full effect, that you may be perfect and complete, lacking in nothing."** —The Bible, James 1:4

10. **"Ask, and it shall be given you."** —The Bible, Matthew 7:7

11. **"Fear not, little flock; for it is your Father's good pleasure to give you the kingdom."** —The Bible, Luke 12:32

12. **"Start by doing what's necessary; then do what's possible; and suddenly you are doing the impossible."**
    —Saint Francis of Assisi

13. **"This too is for the good."** —Nachum Ish Gamzu, Talmud, Taanit 21a

Begin integrating the principles into your life. Then start small, building those manifesting muscles. Once the little things begin demonstrating themselves, choose an area of your life to work on. Schedule time to do this. You may even want to enlist the support of a manifesting buddy, who'd like to create a change themselves, so you can work these processes together. Or simply find an accountability partner. This is a person you make an agreement with to accomplish a specific task. Check in with them to let them know when you do and don't accomplish what was agreed upon. You can even form a book group and work the principles and practices together. What I love most about enlisting others is you get support when challenged and a celebration when succeeding. It feels so good to celebrate!

> God is eternally complete, who directs the stars, who is the master of fates, who elevates man from his lowliness to Himself, who speaks from the cosmos to every single human soul, is the most brilliant manifestation of the goal of perfection.
>
> **—Alfred Adler**

Get a cheap, thick notebook, lined or unlined, your choice. There are so many precious journals out there, with painted and jeweled covers, thick, fancy paper, and ribbon bookmarks. What I've found is their beauty alone invites pressure. Like you can only use them to scribe the Greatest Poem Ever Written. You need a workbook! Something suitable for scribbles, rants, and pages torn out, crumpled and tossed across the room. This is where you will document the laboratory that is your life. Your experiments, failings, and successes. Your ideas and dreams. Your processing. Your affirmations. Let it be an easy container for all of it.

Welcome. Not every practice will work for everyone. But every single reader can grow a more magical, meaningful, and miraculous life using some of what's here. Exaltation awaits!

Getting Started

Beginner's Mind and the Power of Focus

It's likely that this topic of manifestation isn't entirely new to you. In recent years, what was once considered mystical or esoteric has boldly blossomed into mainstream culture. Popular movies, talk shows, and books have urged us over and over again to create the life of our dreams. With social media, we get reminder-memes, with sayings like:

"Whatever you're thinking, you're attracting."

"Keep putting out good. It will come back to you in unexpected ways."

Perhaps you've even tried your hand (or more accurately, your mind) at consciously creating. Whatever your results may have been, from wild success to nothing working, I'm going to encourage you to return to a beginner's mind. This allows you to open to new and perhaps different ideas than you've learned before. The beginner's mind is curious, excited, and ready to start, or start over.

> Don't judge each day by the harvest you reap, but by the seeds that you plant.
> —Robert Louis Stevenson

The Power of Focus

A basic principle of manifesting is that we create more of what we focus on. Even knowing that, you may have noticed, it's just plain easier to focus on problems, what's not working, everything out of place or seemingly out of reach. This is our humanness at work. It's pure biology. The human system is designed to survive, not necessarily thrive. As long as we keep breathing, moving, and eating, the chances for us to reproduce increases, and our species lives on. Fortunately many of us are living in places and cultures where everyday physical survival is not a concern. Your human system does not know this. It has no idea that there is a Starbucks on every corner, awaiting to fuel your caffeine binge. It cares nothing for your soul's fulfilment. It believes your needs could not be met at every possible moment, and it would like you to be hyperaware of that, thank you very much. So if we don't have enough money in our account to pay a bill that has come due, that survival mechanism gets activated. You know logically you will not spontaneously combust if the payment is late. Unfortunately, our human systems are not built for modern life. No matter how hard you try, you can't stop thinking about it. *I can't believe this. I don't get paid until a week*

> We are what we repeatedly do. Excellence, then, is not an act, but a habit.
> —Will Durant

from Friday. And most of that is already spent. I'm going to get hit with a late charge. These thoughts will likely have activated some uncomfortable feelings within you like shame or guilt or even anxiety. You are now consumed with what you don't want to experience more of.

Lack. Scarcity. Life is showing you "not enough" and you're having a difficult time focusing on anything else.

Driven to Distraction

I was an attention deficit disorder (ADD) kid before it had a definition or a name. I would sit for hours each evening at my family's dining room table trying to complete my homework, while my mind bounced from thought to thought. Almost none of these thoughts were on the task before me. I was prone to daydreaming and drifting off, especially when I was bored. Later, on my spiritual path, I could flit around from book to teacher to philosophy, a total workshop junkie, because focus was such a challenge for me. I was forever chasing the next shiny object.

There are two approaches to focus needed for manifesting:

1. **A long, focused session.** You put aside an hour or free afternoon to tackle one or more processes for achieving your goals.

2. **Micro-dosing.** Every day, two or more times per day, you stop, focus, and do a process. It may last one to ten minutes.

Based on what's natural for me, I used to apply the long approach. One of the secrets of being an ADD person is many of us can be hyper-focused for periods of time. Like the building next door is on fire and we don't hear sirens or smell smoke kind of focus. When I fully apply myself to what's before me, I can go for long periods and get a lot done. However, I have found approach number two to be far more effective. Not being a fan of interruptions, this surprised me. Yet several bursts of creative focus made manifesting both faster and easier. And those shorter bursts never added up to the time I would have spent weekly. Regular manifesting reprograms us for success. The long versus the micro-dosing approach can depend on practices. No one is going to create a vision board in five minutes. But once that project is set up, micro-dosing to "work the board" can be a good idea.

It seems like our technological age has inspired ADD-like qualities in just about everyone. We carry around this small device that enables us to read a news story, chat with our Australian friend, apply for a job, share our vacation photos, and answer an email, all within the span of ten minutes. We gather instantaneous responses or reports. Our brains get hooked on all that immediacy. This device has creeped into movie theaters, restaurants, and even our bedrooms. We can't talk about focus without talking about our phones.

Getting Your Smartphone to Work with You Instead of Against You: Set Limits

If your mind keeps drifting to your phone as you try to affirm, meditate, or visualize yourself into a brighter future, manifestation practices won't be as effective as they can be.

1. **Turn it off.** I know. The world may be coming to an end and you're just sitting there, imagining your dream lover, with no way for anyone to contact you. This is where a little trust comes in. Trust that if there's anything you really need to know, the Universe will give you a heads-up. I have certainly gotten divine taps on the shoulder in meditations. And when you live your life moving with the flow of energy, timing just works. You have an inner call receiver that the Universe can utilize at any time. It's what people used in the centuries before phones. This will help stretch your intuition muscles.

   I recommend this for your practices, of course, but not just during your manifesting time. Turn it off when having dinner with a friend. Turn it off at night. Every night or almost. When I mentioned I do this to a friend, she was aghast. "What if there's an emergency and you can't be reached?" I told her I have made it all the way to midlife and there's never been anything that's happened at 3:00 a.m. that it wasn't okay to hear about at 7:00. Now, certain circumstances, like a child attending their first sleepover, or a loved one sick in the hospital, may warrant temporary changes. Make sure those changes are temporary.

   Once you get into a habit of turning your phone off on a regular basis, even if just for ten-minute intervals, I promise it will be a relief to you. It sends a signal to the brain to stop thinking about the phone. Otherwise, part of your awareness is always waiting on the next ping. Now all of you is available. You will need that energy to create.

2. **Change the alert settings.** Recently, a yearly conference I speak at was moved to an online format. Our tech person happened to also be an esteemed colleague who's always full of helpful suggestions. He advised turning off the computer's alerts to both avoid distraction and any embarrassing moments if we were sharing our PowerPoint slides. A private message could pop up while the attendees were viewing the screen. What a revelation! I turned all the alerts off and then did the same for my phone. And kept them turned off! Check your phone's settings for the how-tos.

Using the Smartphone's Features to Your Advantage

1. **The timer.** *Beep!* It's manifesting time! Set the alarm to go off as a reminder to repeat your affirmations or other practices. Maybe you use the same times each day. Or perhaps you set them each morning to work best with a less set schedule. Stop, drop into practice, and roll back to what you were previously doing. You can use the stopwatch to track how much time you've spent practicing.

2. **The camera and photo file.**

   • Take pictures that arouse the feelings you'd like to experience more fully. That may look like what is generally considered inspirational: glowing sunsets, blooming flowers, and light parting pristine clouds in the sky. My phone is filled with many like these. And you may spot an unconventional scene that gives you peace or makes you feel joy. Be open to engaging in the world around you, looking for inspiration everywhere. The key is, not what you think you should be inspired by but what truly positively impacts you. This can be quite unique to you. My camera roll also holds images of urban graffiti, piles of dead leaves, and Vancouver recycling bins. To each their own. Scenic trips offer countless opportunities, and yet so does a regular trip to the supermarket. I like to linger in the produce and flower sections, taking in the colors and textures. And yes, often snapping shots to savor later.

   • Not a picture taker? Welcome to Google images and those of other search engines. Conduct a search. Use the subject of your manifestation. "True love" or "Career in high finance" or

"Healthy body" and see what comes up. Now use feeling words like *freedom, abundance, passion,* and *peace.* Search for a famous person who has manifested what you'd like to create. Play with this and have fun. When you encounter images you love, save them to your phone.

- Create a folder in your phone's photo drive and label it with either a general topic like manifestation or your specific goal. Use the folder title to claim it by starting with the word *My*! "My Ideal Relationship," "My Happy Body," or "My Financial Freedom." Fill it with those inspirational photos. Now include pictures of family, friends, pets, social events, and other joyful elements of your current life. You're blending "what is" with "what will be." This sends powerful messages to this subconscious mind.

- Use the images to focus on what you want. Don't just glance at them, experience them. Take in the colors. Notice the details. What do you love most about each one? The shade of pink in the rose? Your spouse's surprised goofy grin? The way the sun lights up the green hues of the grass?

- Do this . . .

  - While you're experiencing any waiting time at all, like online at the bank or for an actual customer service human to answer your call or checking out at the store. Traffic is great for this as well. As a naturally impatient person living in the most densely populated state in the United States, traffic was maddening for me. Not anymore. I use that time to foster positive, uplifting feelings.

  - While using the restroom. Yes, I said it. You're just sitting there. Might as well get some focusing time in! (You can't say you don't have time for that.)

  - First thing in the morning and before you go to sleep at night. Now this will require a certain amount of discipline. Stick with the pictures, and don't get tempted to jump on social media or check your email. Doing that comes with a high potential for expanding feelings you don't want to experience.

— Show them to a (trusted, supportive) friend. Manifesting can be a delicate business. You're building confidence in yourself, in possibility, in life itself. Choose wisely. Choose a person who believes in you, is open-minded, and would absolutely love to see you succeed. Go through the pictures one by one, saying what you like about them and how they make you feel. Invite them to share a dream they'd like to bring into form. Hope and enthusiasm shared multiplies in surprising ways.

3. **The power in apps.** There are apps for just about everything, including manifesting. Many are free, and most are inexpensive with a free trial period included. Search your phone's app store using the key words: *manifest, law of attraction, affirmations, vision board, gratitude, positive, new thought, inspiration,* and even *goal planner.* When I got my very first smartphone, I downloaded every app on the subject and found them to be creative and fun. And now there are even more to choose from.

Other Ways to Enhance Focus

1. **Exercise.** Particularly in the morning. Getting blood pumping faster through your veins increases clarity.

2. **Spend time in nature.** Being out in the natural world is restorative. It clears out mental clutter and grounds our energy. Whenever possible, take off your shoes and allow your bare feet to touch the ground. After my daily walks, I set up a camping chair, drop the sneakers, take a rest, and connect my energy to the earth. The amount of time depends on the weather. Both the walking and grounding increase my clarity and ability to concentrate.

3. **Sleep.** Sleep. Is. Everything. It affects the most important aspects of daily life, from emotional health to weight to yes, mental processing. Make getting deep, revitalizing sleep a priority.

4. **Limit caffeine.** Most people believe their morning coffee increases focus. But stimulants of all kinds can exacerbate distracted, disordered thinking.

5. **Hydration.** As you're making changes to your thoughts and feelings, you are shifting your energy. Drink plenty of high-quality water to enhance hydration.

You may have noticed these all involve the body. I firmly believe we are spiritual, creative, powerful, limitless beings housed in human experience. When we get our physical bodies in alignment with our spiritual endeavors, including manifesting, everything flows more easily.

> The successful warrior is the average man, with laser-like focus.
> —Bruce Lee

When manifesting, focused efforts bring about clear results. Enhancing your ability to focus will elevate every area of your life. You will have extra time, get more done, and feel a sense of accomplishment. Nurturing that accomplished energy invites more and more of it into your experience.

You'll have an opportunity to do an exercise on this soon.

Take the Quiz: What Kind of Manifestor Are You?

You are manifesting all day, every day, whether you know it or not. The question is, are you manifesting what you want? Take this quiz to see where you may have pitfalls you're not aware of.

And remember, be honest. The only person who sees it is you. If stuck between more than one answer, go with your first thought. It will be a good indication of where your subconscious mind and beliefs are.

1. **You hear about a new position available at work that matches your interests and skills. Your first reaction is:**

   a. Those positions only go to _____ (blondes, boss asskissers, a man, someone younger, those with higher degrees, etc.).

   b. If I go for this, I'll just mess it up.

   c. I definitely want this. It's more money, more visibility. But what if it's more hours? And I can't keep up? But maybe I can? I don't know!

   d. I can imagine how good this would be!

   e. I have the skills and will start putting a manifestation plan into motion now.

2. **When something unpleasant happens unexpectedly . . .**

   a. I'm not surprised. What else can you expect in this crappy world?

   b. I blame myself. I must have caused this. Nothing ever works in my favor.

   c. I get upset, try to talk myself out of it, and waver on its meaning for me.

   d. I ignore the upset and know this must have happened for a reason.

   e. I pay attention to the feelings, allow them to flow, process if needed, and return to focusing on what I want versus what I don't want.

3. **You get an idea on a new business venture. What happens next?**

   a. I give up almost immediately. The economy is a mess after all!

   b. I think of all the times I failed in the past. What if that happens again? Better not to even try.

   c. I immediately start researching online. Read about the percentages of new businesses failing. Give up. Then spend the next year wondering if it could have worked.

   d. I imagine how good it would feel to run my own successful business! I think about the perfect wardrobe and see myself as winning, telling friends how much I love this. I just never go any further.

   e. I begin imagining how this could be, affirm its happening, then begin researching, quickly finding the right resources and praying for, and looking for signs of divine timing. I get a promising lead and follow up on it.

4. **What best describes your parents' / primary caregivers' most persistent outlook on life? If you grew up in a two-parent household and they held different views, respond with the caregiver whose views were more dominant or present.**

   a. It's an unfair world. Get used to it.

b. You/I can never do anything right.

c. You're not sure how they viewed life. You received a lot of mixed messages.

d. They wore rose-colored glasses; looking for the good while ignoring the bad.

e. It's hard to remember because you focus on your outlook and beliefs, not theirs.

5. **You want to make a healthy change. How much do you trust yourself to implement it?**

a. Not at all. Why bother?

b. Not much. I don't have a good track record.

c. Somewhat.

d. I'll think about it!

e. I can do it.

6. **Your friend mentions having always wanted to visit Paris, a city you'd like to see yourself, and wants to start planning a trip. From what you know, her finances aren't in the best place. How do you respond?**

a. I don't say anything. I know she can't pull it off.

b. I don't say anything, because I don't want her to get her hopes up, only to be disappointed.

c. I encourage her only to follow up with several questions like, "How will you afford that?"

d. You tell her you know she can do it! Anything is possible! You just don't think to go as well.

e. You ask if you can come along and start envisioning an ideal place to stay, perfect weather, and a joyous good time. Then you speak to your friend about each of you setting up a separate savings account with a specific dollar amount goal for each month.

7. **"I believe anything is possible." How true is this statement for you?**

   a. Ninety-nine percent untrue, I mean, seriously?

   b. True for others but not for me.

   c. Fifty-fifty.

   d. One hundred percent true! I just don't have anything to back that up!

   e. Almost always true when dreams are in alignment with supportive beliefs, inspired action, balanced energy, and a soul's purpose.

8. **Think of the last time you received something you really wanted (e.g., an offer, a gift, a service). How long ago was it?**

   a. Huh?

   b. I don't know, but I got my friend something she really wanted for her birthday.

   c. Six months or longer, I think, but I'm not sure.

   d. Not recently, but it could happen at any time!

   e. Less than six months.

9. **If you could wave a magic wand and accomplish one thing, what would you choose:**

   a. End horrific injustice for anyone marginalized (people of color, women, animals).

   b. Help people in my community who don't have enough to eat.

   c. There are too many choices. It's overwhelming!

   d. World peace.

   e. A world that works for everyone, in which all people are safe, healthy, prosperous, loved, accepted, and free to be their true selves.

10. **You're invited to a celebratory social gathering. First thoughts?**

    a. *Ugh. There probably won't be anyone I know there. I wonder how soon I can leave. I probably shouldn't go.*

    b. *I hope the other people there like me.*

    c. You think of five reasons to attend and five reasons not to.

    d. *Wow! It's going to be a good time.*

    e. You check in with yourself, think about what you'd like to have happen there. This could be a good opportunity to feel joyful and make new friends.

11. **How much of your time is spent thinking of the past, whether that was decades ago or yesterday?**

    a. Often. There's been so much unfairness.

    b. Often. There have been so many regrets.

    c. My thinking is all over the place—past, present, and future.

    d. Not much. I mostly think of the future.

    e. Depends. I focus on the past when I am cleaning up old memories and beliefs. I use the present to focus on what I'd like my future to be.

12. **Your coworker snaps at you. How personally do you take it?**

    a. Not at all. F her! (But you seethe about it for days, plotting your revenge.)

    b. Very! I'll do anything to make up for whatever I did wrong. (Then spend weeks walking on eggshells around her.)

    c. It's probably just her. But maybe I did do something too? (You debate this over and over again in your own head.)

    d. Not at all. I'll just send her love and light! (You are extra kind while ignoring your own reaction.)

    e. Everyone's having a human experience, including her. I'll check in with her later and then let this go. (Finding compassion, addressing it, and releasing.)

13. Waking from a beautiful dream about being in love with a mystery partner, you think:

    a. *It was just a dream. Dreams don't mean anything.*

    b. *That won't happen for me.*

    c. *Do dreams have any meaning? Or are they just nonsense? I'm not sure.*

    d. *It's a sign! Love will happen for me!*

    e. *I'm going to savor these yummy love feelings and know this is happening for me.*

14. What's your spirit animal?

    a. A crow.

    b. A donkey.

    c. An otter.

    d. A butterfly.

    e. An eagle.

15. There's an extended family member who pushes all your buttons. You're seeing him tomorrow. What do you do?

    a. Cancel. Who needs the drama?

    b. Blame myself.

    c. Spend the entire evening trying to decide and asking everyone I know for advice.

    d. Go. It will be fine. We are all God's children!

    e. Visualize how you'd like the day to go and affirm feeling good.

16. Someone you love is heartbroken. What do you do?

    a. Show up with ice cream and five shocking stories about my exes.

    b. Show up and spend the night apologizing like I did something wrong.

c. Show up and can't decide what to do. Drag her to a party? Give her tissues?

d. Show up and tell her it's for the best, everything happens for a reason, and she is beautiful.

e. On your own, you pray for her and send her loving energy. Then you show up, hold her hand, listen, express compassion, and remind her this too shall pass.

17. **You have a free weekend. How do you spend it?**

a. Stalking former friends on social media, catching up on news, and watching scary movies.

b. Trying to find someone, anyone, to hang out with!

c. Spend all of Saturday trying to make up my mind.

d. Frisbee in the park, making new friends, and listening to upbeat music.

e. I start with morning spiritual practices, focus on how I want to feel, and choose activities I believe will support that.

18. **You find yourself in a group conversation with unfamiliar people. How do you respond?**

a. I go silent. I don't know if I can trust them.

b. I don't say much. I don't want to sound stupid.

c. Out of nervousness, I talk a lot, then fall silent to see how people are reacting to me.

d. I compliment almost every single person and share how excited I am to be speaking with them.

e. I'm open to what I'm hearing, and if any topic comes up that I resonate with, I share my insight.

19. **You get cut off in traffic. How do you react?**

a. Curse, beep the horn, and follow up closely behind them.

b. Shrink back. I was probably going too slowly.

    c. Get flustered.

    d. Ignore my racing heart and send them love and light.

    e. Think, *They could be on their way to the hospital,* take a deep breath, let it out, and affirm, "I am safe."

20. **When faced with a decision, what normally happens?**

    a. Imagine the worst and ignore it until it goes away.

    b. Go with what's the least risky/scary.

    c. You really struggle with making decisions.

    d. Immediately do whatever. Things always work out.

    e. Check in with my inner guidance, then act accordingly.

21. **After watching a movie that moved you, what happens next?**

    a. Immediately forget about it. It's just a movie.

    b. Doubt anything good like that could happen for me. That only happens in movies.

    c. Try to find something else to watch. There are too many choices.

    d. Focus on all the good stuff I liked.

    e. Examine it for deeper meaning and relive the scenes I liked best in my imagination.

22. **Where is your attention most often?**

    a. On the past. On everything that has happened to me.

    b. On the past. On everything I did wrong.

    c. My attention is all over the place.

    d. The future. It's gonna be so bright, I gotta wear shades!

    e. Using my present to create a good future. The present gives me important information on what I really want and what I need to release to get there.

23. **I'm normally very clear about what I'm feeling. How true is this?**

    a. Yeah, miserable!

    b. Yes, invisible.

    c. No, my feelings change so fast it's hard to keep up.

    d. Of course, life is good. What's not to love?

    e. I take the time to journal my feelings because I know they are pointing me where to go and where not to go.

24. **When you daydream, the topic is most often . . .**

    a. Revenge.

    b. A damsel in distress being saved.

    c. It's like flipping through several TV channels.

    d. Everyone loves me.

    e. I consciously direct them to what I'm actively creating at the time.

25. **What are your thoughts on five-year plans?**

    a. I don't think past next week.

    b. They make me sad.

    c. Why five years? Why not two or ten?

    d. I'm in love with my dream partner, fabulously wealthy, and living on a yacht.

    e. I write down my goals for each area of my life and begin manifesting it, leaving room for something even better.

26. **Your feelings on technology most often are . . .**

    a. When are the robots taking over?

    b. I can't keep up.

    c. It's all so confusing.

    d. We can connect to anyone in the world.

    e. Finding ways for technology to make my life better.

27. **You had an upsetting conversation with your partner. How long after it's over do you think about it?**

    a. Every. Damn. Day.

    b. All the time. I want to be able to fix it.

    c. Often when I have downtime.

    d. Not at all. The past is the past.

    e. Address any deeper issues and then move on. I'm not a dweller.

28. **Something you were really planning on happening falls through. What do you think?**

    a. Figures. That's the way things go in this messed-up world.

    b. I'm not surprised. *Disappointment* is my middle name.

    c. I don't know what to think!

    d. It's all good. It wasn't meant to be.

    e. Release any hard feelings, recommit to the vision, and trust in divine timing.

29. **You make a mistake.**

    a. It's not my fault!

    b. It's all my fault.

    c. What did I do wrong?

    d. There are no mistakes in the big picture of life.

    e. Mistakes are important growth opportunities. Get the wisdom, course correct, and keep going.

30. **A friend wants to fix you up with a person who seems to have it all. What do you say?**

    a. Is their type sullen?

    b. They'll never go for me.

    c. Ask a hundred questions about their past romantic life.

    d. Imagine marrying them.

e. Face any insecurities, then go forward with a sincere intention to look for the good and have a fun time.

Score:

Add up the numbers you got for each letter.

A _____

B _____

C _____

D _____

E _____

If you scored mostly As, you're likely a:
REALITY BIG-TIME BITER

Your focus is on all the "bad" that has happened in the past and happening now, both in your own life and in the suffering you see in the world. This is an easy place to get stuck in your creative process. Creating what you want feels frivolous, selfish, and that it won't make a difference in the big picture. You may feel consumed with the constant news cycle, adding mental evidence to all that isn't fair. You may have equated the idea of manifestation or even a general belief in something greater than yourself to checked-out, science-denying, kale-smoothy-drinking, conspiracy-loving bliss bunnies. For you, it's imperative you understand that everything is connected, so any big-picture changes you'd like to see can only happen when many people make internal changes. Living an empowered life inside allows you to be a bigger change agent outside. Once you're earning the money you'd like, you can donate to causes that are making a significant difference. Or take time off to volunteer. Remember that every university, hospital, and museum that exists was likely funded by a small group of wealthy people. Become one of those!

If you scored mostly Bs, you're likely a:
DOUBLE-DOWN DOUBTER

You doubt your ability to create what you want and the Universe's ability to deliver it to you. You may have tried to create what you wanted in the past and gotten easily discouraged, giving up before the creation was complete. You're protecting yourself from a fear of disappointment and fostering feelings of low self-esteem. You imagine everything that can go wrong while disregarding what could go right. You want to maintain control so you'll get a guaranteed outcome before proceeding. But on some level, that's not how the creative process works. For you, building confidence in yourself and the Universe will be key. Starting small on your manifesting journey will help you to slowly build to taking larger risks with your deepest desires. And start affirming your self-worth now, even if it feels ridiculous. In time, that will change.

If you scored mostly Cs, you're likely a:
WISHY-WASHY WAFFLER

You think you can have this. You want this. Then you don't. Then you do. Maybe. You start out strong, create a plan, and even tell your inner circle you're going to make this happen, only to find your enthusiasm quickly fizzles out while falling back into bad habits. Easily distracted, you may begin chasing the next dream while abandoning the current project. The problem is, soon after, the next dream will be abandoned as well. Lack of consistency and indecisiveness are your biggest weaknesses. For you, making a firm decision and sticking to it will likely flush out those bad habits or unconscious beliefs that are getting in your way. If in the process of manifesting something, you get bored, rededicate yourself to this goal anyway. Find the passionate feelings for it once again. If this doesn't work, journal about what's in the way.

If you scored mostly Ds, you're likely a:
PROPRIETOR OF POSSIBILITIES

You believe in what could be. You're open to more good. You're an excellent cheerleader and supporter of other people's dreams and goals. "You got this!" If I looked at your social media page, I'd see a whole lot of positivity. But your outer life has not changed. Your career, relationships, and bank account have stayed much the same. For you, the culprit is staying in the fantasy of what's possible, rather than taking action to bring it into form. It's important for you to move from the feel-good, lovely daydreaming to taking real, inspired action. Make sure you don't get stuck in the invisible and make what you want visible.

If you scored mostly Es, you're likely a:
CONCENTRATED COCREATOR

You work with the conscious mind to focus on what you want, pay attention to intuition and inspiration, and take inspired action without delay. You've created a home and lifestyle that support your desires and well-being. When doubts and fears arise, you face them directly and use powerful tools to neutralize them. Once you've reached this place, the question to ask yourself is, "Am I thinking big enough?" It may be time to move up to the next level!

If you had mixed results, with similar high numbers in more than one category:

Inconsistency is your sworn enemy. Get clear about your blind spots, clean them up, and move forward.

For a printable version of this quiz, visit www.manifestingbook.com.

The Manifesting Alchemy Contract

Why a Contract?

Contracts exist for very important reasons. They are agreements that define a desired result, the means to creating it, the time frame for completion, and the repercussions for not doing so. You wouldn't think of having your kitchen remodeled or website created

> It is not only what we do, but also what we do not do, for which we are accountable.
> —Molière

without one. If the idea of a contract with yourself feels rigid or stifling, then I'm going to strongly encourage you to try this. Conscious creation requires your commitment and a foundation on which inspiration can build. Think of the contract not as a punishing tool but a concrete reminder on how to best rise up for yourself and your desires.

How to Use It

1. **Times.** Create a definite start and end time. This is the time frame in which you will do the practices outlined, not for the manifestation to happen. To build self-confidence, particularly if you feel you haven't lived up to commitments you've made to yourself in the past, start small. What can you commit to doing for a week? After that week is complete, create a new contract and expand the time frame.

2. **Areas.** Choose one area in your life to start manifesting.

3. **What You Want.** Write briefly about what you'd like to experience in this area. I say *briefly* because you will be getting clearer, refining and perhaps even redefining as the process unfolds.

4. **Practices.** Choose a practice (or two or three) you feel drawn to and can help you get focused and feel the feelings of this creation.

5. **Duration.** Agree to a duration for these practices. Daily, weekly, monthly. Ten minutes or an hour. This will vary according to the practices themselves and your schedule. I strongly encourage you to create time for these activities. Think of the time you spend online and watching TV. Use some of that for creating. And don't overschedule with these activities either. If you make it arduous, you'll soon find reason not to do it! Get specific and use a timer.

> Accountability and self-responsibility are critical to our success in personal, professional and public life. However, we often look for those character traits in others, rather than inculcating them in ourselves.
>
> —**Vishwas Chavan**

6. **Repercussions.** Just like with any contract, if you don't do what is agreed, there will be penalties. Perhaps you donate to a favorite charity or add twenty minutes to your daily walk. Maybe you forgo TV for a week. When you don't meet a commitment to yourself, the repercussions are not punishments but rather another opportunity to now keep your word. They should be strong enough that you feel them, but do choose healthy and life-affirming penalties over anything self-abusive.

This is extremely important. If you recognize you didn't honor the contract, be kind to yourself, then follow up on the consequences. Do not use this process to think or speak harshly to yourself.

7. **Affirmations.** Use the contract to affirm your worthiness and ability to do this!

8. **Signature and Witness.** Sign and print your name. Can I get a witness? Yes, get a (kind, supportive) witness to read this contract and sign along with you. It adds more power when we say not just to ourselves but another, *I am going to do this.* You may want to make this person an accountability partner.

Manifesting Alchemy Contract

Start Date _____ End Date _____

Today, I, _____(full name), have made a firm decision.

    I commit to manifesting what I desire in this area of my life: _____ (money, career, health, relationships, creative self-expression, achievements, projects, etc.)

I am manifesting:

_____

_____

To create this, I commit to the following manifestation practice(s) for alchemy to flourish in my life. I do these for the times indicated:

    Practice and Duration

- _____

- _____

- _____

If I don't complete this commitment, the repercussion is:

_____

_____

I declare:

All "setbacks" are actually opportunities to dissolve doubts and keep going!

I declare that I am worthy of having this!

I have everything I need within me to accomplish this!

I am One with a loving Universe that says *yes* to my desires!

This is unfolding perfectly in my life now!

Signature: _____

Date: _____

Print Name:_____

Witness:

Signature: _____

Date: _____

Print Name:_____

For a printable version of this contract,
visit www.manifestingbook.com.

PART ONE

The 7 Powerful Manifesting Alchemy Principles

1

Manifesting Alchemy Principle 1

FOCUSING ON THE GOOD

As a manifestor, it's always important to practice stretching your focusing muscles. Just like stretching your physical body is valuable to do before exercise.

I once lived in an apartment that had nonstop plumbing issues. Every few days, in utter frustration, we'd plead with our landlord. He'd call the plumber, who would arrive in a maroon work van. Often I'd sit on the front porch waiting for the cavalry to arrive, for that maroon van. After that, I began seeing maroon vans everywhere. Each time, I'd think, *That must be our plumber,* and pull up alongside only to find it never was. It just seemed like our entire town was suddenly overrun with the exact kind of maroon van he drove. I had focused on the van so intensely, I not only trained myself to see them but was also attracting them into my experience. Once the repairs were finally

> What you get by achieving your goals is not as important as what you become by achieving your goals.
> —Zig Ziglar

completed, I stopped looking for the vans, and they stopped showing up on the road in front of me. It was a great lesson for me.

Now's your turn to experiment with the power of focus. Have fun with this.

Focus

1. **Start small.** When you begin consciously creating, start with things that are unimportant and in which you have zero attachment. Pick anything that feels random. Here are a few ideas:

   - Monarch butterflies

   - Bananas

   - Mason jars

   - A black camera

   - Rainbows

   - A three-digit number that has no meaning for you, like 752

   - Overhanging Edison lights

   - Vintage typewriters

2. **Spend a few minutes focusing on this item.** See it. Imagine touching it. Tracing the outlines of it.

3. **Print out an image of this item and place it in your wallet.** Place another copy of the image beside your bed and look at it each morning and night. Put another on your refrigerator and one in your car on the passenger seat. If you don't have a printer, put it on your phone's wallpaper so you see it each time you pick it up.

4. **Document what happens.** Make a mental note each time you see this item.

   For the monarch butterfly example, one may land on your

shoulder. Then you see an image tattooed on a woman's ankle. Next, a child walks by you with monarch butterflies on his shirt. A friend sends you a link to a news story about monarch butterflies growing in numbers. You begin to see that what you focus on expands. Even something as random as a butterfly.

This experiment works so easily because you don't have an attachment to or beliefs about butterflies. You don't think that you're undeserving of them. No one told you when you were growing up that people like you never see butterflies. You didn't lose your butterflies in the divorce.

After you've seen what simple focusing can do, let's start on something that brings a benefit to you.

Because, after all, who needs to see a bunch of maroon vans? They're not exactly car eye candy.

Begin using your focusing abilities for more of what you actually want to see and experience.

Potential Targets

- The right parking space at the perfect time.*

- Late reservations at a busy restaurant.

- A sale on a smaller much-wanted item or the money to purchase it full price. (Think toaster versus new car for now.)

- Tickets to a popular show.

Apply the Same Practices

- Imagine having it. Arouse the feelings it will bring you.

---

*A word on parking spaces. These are not always frivolous manifestations. Once, I slipped on black ice and threw out my lower back. Needing to see my acupuncturist ASAP, I manifested a spot directly in front of her office, in the center of a busy downtown area known for its nonexistent parking. I could hardly walk. This spot meant I could get very necessary treatment.

- Surround yourself with images of it.

- Document what happens.

If you begin to waver, imagine it's a pizza. You want a pizza, you order it, and just expect it will be delivered. You don't wonder if the pizza will arrive. You don't think, *Well, there's so much traffic today. The pizza may not make it.* Or, *So many people want pizza. There may not be enough for me.* Release the attachment and allow it to flow into your experience.

Focusing on the Good

There is good in your life and in all life. I don't know you, and yet I can say this without hesitation. If you have a safe place to live, food in your kitchen, people who love you, and access to the internet, you have the world. Your physical and social needs are being met, and the internet can be a source of your education, connection, and entertainment.

> When you focus on being the best person you can be, you draw the best possible life, love, and opportunities to you.
>
> **—Germany Kent**

Look for the Good in Every Person and Every Situation

This is simple, but not easy.

Internally, we have survival minds and nervous systems designed to spot trouble. Externally, we are living in times when society is actually addicted to fear and major catastrophes. It's ever unfolding in our social and news media. And we are absolutely immersed in all forms of media. Gone are the days of the 6:00 news. It's quite easy to fall down the well of "ain't it awful."

It's important to take control of your thoughts and direct them to ways that make you happy. I'm not asking you to pretend here. I'm asking you to legitimately focus on the good in people and circumstances.

What's "Right" Right Now?

Loving the Good

1. List the primary people in your life.

2. Begin with the folks with whom you have the most positive relationships.

3. Write down everything you appreciate about them. Start with the obvious, then go deeper.

4. Now begin this process on anyone you might be struggling with right now. Where is the good in them? Even if you find them challenging, how are they in other relationships? What good can you see in their employment?

You may even be able to find good in an area of disagreement.

For example, your brother is very religious and puts down your spiritual beliefs. Even though they are not yours, what good is there in his beliefs? Maybe they cause him to donate money where it's truly needed. Or have helped him stop drinking. Or inspired him to be a better father.

I have done this practice time and time again with people I am challenged by. And I continue to be amazed at the results.

With one such person, for a very long time, the best I could find was: "She wears cool shoes."

But after I'd see her, I'd return to the list again.

"She wears cool shoes."

"She's got good posture."

"I like her passion for her family. You can tell she really loves them."

> If you look the right way, you see the whole world is a garden.
>
> —Frances Hodgson Burnett

The list would grow each time, and the more it did, the easier it was to be around her. The easier it was to be around her, the gentler she became. The gentler she became, the more I could see her intelligence and wit. The relationship changed completely. She is not the only person this has happened with.

Develop a daily practice for focusing on what's right, good, and beautiful. Here's an example of consciously shifting focus.

You and your partner leave a party. The hostess is a good friend, but you find her spouse insufferable. Normally, you'd spend the drive home laughing about every time he bragged, interrupted, or dominated the conversation. You honestly have no idea how she stands him! Usually, the focus of conversation would be on him. From there, it would likely spiral into the fact you had to park ten blocks away, there were too many unfamiliar people, and you honestly would have preferred to stay home.

Instead, turn the conversation to all that was right. You loved your friend's dress. The food was delicious and healthy. Isn't it nice to go to a party where the food is so thoughtfully prepared? You'd really like that vegan potato salad recipe. It was so interesting speaking with your friend's coworker on her time in the Peace Corps. The music mix was the perfect blend of upbeat without being overpowering. You were so happy they set up extra chairs so you didn't have to stand all night. They must have put a lot of energy, time, and money into creating a very special evening. You remember to call her tomorrow and thank her.

It's the same evening. You didn't somehow rewind time and change anything that occurred. Upon reflection, you decided to bring a very different mindset to the experience. As you started to delve, you realized that so much good had been there after all.

And here you are, beloved reader, taking in two perspectives on an imaginary scenario. How did you feel reading about the insufferable spouse? Remind you of anyone? I bet it did because we all know someone like that! Next, you read the positive review. How did that feel, just in reading it? I bet a whole lot better. Calmer. More peaceful. Like maybe you'd enjoy an invite to just such an event. All from a party that did not even happen!

If you have a partner, you may think they will never go along with it. Try it anyway. Without a lecture. No "Honey, I think tonight we should focus on all the wonderful aspects of the party instead of scrutinizing Jim." That will bring up resistance. Your partner could feel wronged for a behavior you both engaged in. Don't take the bait. Just gently counter your partner's complaints with one of your positive observations. Ask questions based on those. "I really enjoyed the food. Did you try the potato salad? How did you like it? What did you like best?" Even if your partner does not share your opinions, they will be able to access the good vibes. You alone can shift the energy into an upward rise. Just keep focusing on the good and sharing it with enthusiasm.

Upgrade Your Reviews

We live in a time where almost everything gets reviewed, from restaurants to Uber drivers to dentists. The internet has given everyone a voice. Too often it's used to criticize rather than compliment. It's time for a much-needed upgrade.
It's time for you to review!

1. **In your journal, pick something from the day before to review.** It could be anything at all. Your evening commute. The salad you had for lunch. That meeting. The selection of flowers at the supermarket. The museum visit. The movie.

2. **Set a timer for three minutes.**

3. **Quickly write down every single thing you liked about it.**

4. **Bonus:** If what you're reviewing is something for which there's a place for posting, do so. Spread some of that love around!

This exercise has dual purposes. First, you're focusing on the good. Check! Next, because you have this daily assignment, you'll be more present in those experiences. You'll open the salad asking, *What's good about this?* Instead of choking it down, you'll savor it. You'll enter the supermarket seeking the positives, so you'll have something to write down. Now you're not only experiencing the good upon reflection but in the present moment as well. The more you do this, the better your everyday experiences become. It's easy to find the good during vacation; after all, that's the purpose for going on one. Imagine bringing that awareness to the everyday. You can make the supermarket your next vacation.

> I can live for two months on a good compliment.
>
> —**Mark Twain**

7 Ways to Remind Yourself of Your Worth Every Day

1. **Leave Post-it love notes for yourself.**
   On the bathroom mirror. In your desk drawer. On the light fixture over the kitchen table. On the steering wheel of your car. Everywhere!

2. **Make note of daily successes.**
   Open up your definition of success. Some days, paying a bill on time is a huge success. On another, you may have gotten accolades from a trusted colleague. If you have the flu, success will look like taking a shower. Recognize them all.

3. **Choose to be kind.**
   Especially when it isn't easy. When we respond from our best selves, take the high road, and lead with compassion, we feel better about ourselves.

4. **Help someone.**
   Especially when you yourself are feeling helpless. Find anyone you can give support to. You realize how powerful you are to make a difference in another's life.

5. **Affirm it.**
   "I am worthy of all good. I am a beloved child of the Universe. I deserve and embrace freedom and joy."

6. **Create.**
   Write a poem. Paint. Make an altar of sacred objects. Retile the bathroom. Create an online club for a passionate interest. Where there was once nothing, now there is *this. You* did that!

7. **Hug yourself.**
   Seriously. Wrap your arms around yourself, breathing deeply, and feel being both the giver and receiver of love.

2

Manifesting Alchemy Principle 2

STOP WAITING

t took me years to realize this.

For much of my life, I perpetually put myself in a state of waiting. Once I was done waiting for one thing, it would be replaced by waiting for something else. When I worked in social services, it was waiting for the next paid holiday, weekend, or vacation. When I wasn't in a relationship, it was waiting for the things I would do with "him," whoever he was going to be. There was waiting until I lost weight (wait/weight, interesting, huh?), and waiting until I became _____ (less anxious, more enlightened, more successful) to ease up, to be happy, to finally love myself. All it did was perpetuate more and more waiting. There was never a finish line. I was always moving the baton further and further ahead while I struggled to catch it. It constantly

> Don't wait. The time will never be just right.
> —Napoleon Hill

fed an energy of not having, not being good enough, and a total lack of appreciation for all I did indeed have. As a person with no patience whatsoever, this was maddening.

Whenever you're seeking to create anything, stop waiting to experience the happiness you believe the manifestation will provide. Start creating the happiness right now.

I thought I needed a man to buy a house. Isn't that how it's supposed to work? Isn't that what I was told in movies and media? I kept waiting on Mr. Right to fulfill this dream. Sadly, decades of modern evidence to the contrary had not breached that belief in me. When I realized I was delaying my good, I decided to stop waiting. Many thought it couldn't be done. After all, I live in an area with very high housing costs and taxes. And I was on a social service salary at the time, no less. It didn't matter. I was determined, and I knew that I could create what I wanted.

> Never allow waiting to become a habit. Live your dreams and take risks. Life is happeneing now.
>
> —Paulo Coelho

I first spoke with a real estate agent a friend introduced me to. I told him what I wanted. A two-bedroom house with a yard within a fifteen-minute commute to my job. He literally scoffed. "Oh no, just no. You will never be able to find that with what you've been approved for! Not in this area. And what do you want with a house anyway? You're single. I have a few condos I'll show you." And that was both the beginning and end of our professional relationship. I knew if he didn't believe it was possible for me to get what I wanted, it would not happen. I needed an agent who was on the same page. The next one said, "Oh, we can find that for you!" And we did. I learned of special mortgages for lower-income people that had many benefits, including a lower down payment and no PMI. I was quickly approved. As I sat down with the lawyer on signing day, he said, "This is a really, really good interest rate. I haven't seen anyone in my office with an interest rate this low in years. Oh, this is a nice-size property. And the yard. That's a good-size yard! For this amount? In this town? I've never seen anything like this."

The funny thing is, after I bought the house, I met a tall, handsome, smart, and funny guy, and we had a happy, long-term relationship for many years. It didn't happen in the order I expected. But it did indeed happen.

What Are You Waiting For?

Think of all the areas of creation. Money, career, love, friendships, life goals. What do you believe needs to happen first for you to have what you want?

Fill in the blanks:

When I have _____,
then I will _____ .

When I get _____,
then I will _____ .

When I achieve _____,
then I will _____ .

When I create _____,
then I will _____ .

When I receive _____,
then I will _____ .

When I accomplish _____,
then I will _____ .

When I earn _____,
then I will _____ .

Complete this sentence for each goal you'd like to achieve. Feel free to list multiple options for all that you're waiting on.
   Some examples:

- When I earn more money, then I'll travel to Bali.

- When I have the right relationship, then I'll take the Circle Line cruise around New York City and visit that new Brazilian restaurant.

- When I receive my next promotion, then I'll hire a cleaning service and finally buy a new couch.

- When I create more time, then I'll write a book and learn yoga.

Don't wait. Create these outcomes or something similar now.

In the example of Bali, maybe you don't have the money right now, in this moment, to travel there. Start researching. Join a Facebook group for Bali travelers. Read up on its history and weather patterns. Find the ten things you must absolutely do while in Bali! Learn to cook Balinese dishes. Purchase a piece of native art. Speak to a person who has been there and interview them about their experience. Watch YouTube videos that feature this island.

And then travel to a place you can afford. Any place new. Even if it's just that museum in the town next door you've never visited. Make it an adventure!

If you're single, find friends who are willing to share the experiences you've previously reserved for the One. No, sipping champagne with an upbeat coworker isn't exactly the same as it would be with the love of your life. But it's still pretty darn good! And if you've ever been on what you thought would be a dream date, only to have your partner show up distracted, grumpy, or unwell, then you know it's not necessarily the person, but the disposition that makes the experience.

Turning Associations Around

We make associations between two or more unrelated things in our minds all the time. Like a food association is a cheeseburger with french fries. They are lumped together so frequently, we think this is how it's supposed to be. I'll never forget when a friend practically melted down at a restaurant that served its burgers only with salads. "This is simply an atrocity, Kris!" she wailed.

"An *atrocity*?" I countered as I started to laugh. But that's how firmly associations can become entrenched. Think of them as attachments that can get in your way.

With waiting, we've made an association between the manifestation and what will unfold after its arrival. When we engage in the outcomes first, that which we've been putting off "until" sends signals to the Universe that we're ready now for the manifestation. Use the associations to your advantage and experience now what is within your control.

> If you are the kind of person who is waiting for the "right" thing to happen, you might wait for a long time. It's like waiting for all the traffic lights to be green for five miles before starting the trip.
>
> **—Robert Kiyosaki**

Waiting Versus Quiet Expectation

The energy of waiting feels irritating, impatient, and jumpy. If you ever were left waiting for a loved one to arrive for a special event, you know these feelings. But what if every arrival happened right on time? Maybe not on human time but divine time. Now imagine the energy of quiet expectancy. You know it's coming. You know it will unfold in perfect timing. It simply *is* happening so you trust it will arrive right on time. And you softly open your arms to embrace it, whenever that is. This feels gentle, patient, welcoming, and relaxed.

Transform your waiting energy into this.

Affirm:

"Everything is unfolding in divine timing."

"I am relaxed and ready to receive."

"I trust all is unfolding in perfect order now."

"I release any pressure and embrace the grace of the Universe. All is well."

Manifesting Reflection Questions

1. **Think of something you've been waiting on for a long time.** Write down the thoughts you think when this comes to mind.

2. How would your life be different if you stopped waiting? What actions would you take?

3. How would life be different if you trusted the Universe?

4. How would you feel if you knew you could have your deepest desires?

Manifesting Alchemy Principle 3

DESERVABILITY AND OPEN RECEIVING

've been on this planet long enough to observe that those who feel deserving of good usually have it. Or more appropriately, I could say they are most successful in creating it. This perpetual magnetic vibe emanates from their beings, saying, "Yes, life, I deserve all this and more, more, more." You can be annoyed with those people, or you can become one of them. Trust me, for much of my life, encounters with these folks left me disgruntled and bitter. "They're so selfish. It's all about them!" That is, until I decided to become one myself. And lo and behold, I have so

> Whatever you accomplish in life is a manifestation not as much of what you do, as of what you believe you deserve.
> —Les Brown

much more to give now than I ever did before. This is an important vibe to cultivate within yourself.

Now, there are a lot of reasons why we don't feel deserving. There are beliefs in the collective consciousness about class, gender, sexual orientation, geographical location, age, and much more. Regardless of what's happening "out there," you can only create change from the inside out. As we are all connected, what's happening in the world does have an effect on us when we are living unconsciously—that is, until we make empowered choices and start creating from within rather than living the effects of the collective.

Get rid of any old programming that's weighing you down. See chapter 24, "Dealing with Doubts and Releasing Resistance."

> When you get to a place where you understand that love and belonging, your worthiness, is a birthright and not something you have to earn, anything is possible.
>
> **—Brené Brown**

And if you've been waiting for someone to come along and say, "You deserve good!" then please, by all means, allow that person to be me.

You are a spark of divine life-force energy. There will never be another unique you. You are deserving of a life worth rejoicing over. You don't help anyone or the world by being less. You are worthy to create and embrace a life that makes your heart sing with purpose and joy. You aren't just loved. You are love itself, in human form, here to create heaven on earth. At conception, one out of millions of sperm joined an egg and created you, the result that is the winning combination. Know this, and allow it to become your truth.

Now I'm going to speak to those of you who may be observing current social trends toward narcissism and hubris. You think, *No way! I don't want to be like that.* Let me be clear. Healthy self-esteem and feeling worthy of a beautiful life will never look like unbridled greed, obsessive pettiness, or shallow vanity. Narcissists and others like them are actually deeply insecure, easily swayed by others' opinions, and very much disempowered. This is not self-love. When you cultivate love and deservability from the inside out, you're living life from your true power, your spiritual essence.

Start stretching your worthiness for good by becoming an open receiver.

Receiving with Grace and Appreciation

You'd like to receive more good from the Universe. It's important to lovingly receive what is being given right now. Life has a multitude of good bestowers at its disposal. Right now, it may look like money in the parking meter you just pulled up to. Next week, it could be a delicious dinner.

And a year from now, it may be a prosperous job offer. Best get your receiving muscles toned now.

When you give too much and don't receive enough, it can make you feel resentful and depleted. Nothing kills money mojo more than seething resentment.

Receiving

What to Receive

1. **Compliments.** These can be difficult for many. You're being acknowledged for anything from the stellar outfit you're wearing to a major accomplishment like earning a degree. Instead of beaming with healthy pride, you find yourself shrinking instead. There can be many reasons for this. Perhaps you were raised to believe it's better to give than receive. (Both are equally necessary. See Manifesting Alchemy Principle 4 starting on page 69.) Maybe a compliment makes you feel like you're temporarily in the spotlight and you don't like the attention. The discomfort could be triggering a troublesome belief or distorted self-image. Please know, these can be healed. For now, remember this: when you decline a compliment, you are insulting the giver and shutting down your energetic flow. Stop, smile, say a sincere thank-you, let the compliment in, and breathe into any discomfort until it passes.

2. **Valuable advice.** Admittedly, this is tricky. We're all being inundated with "Ya know what you need to do?" about a hundred times a day. And now you're reading a book where on every page, I'm saying, "You know what would work is . . ." The key word here is *valuable.* From stock portfolio tips to health regimens to yes, even operating instructions for Universal Abundance, if you've been given worthwhile advice, receive it. How will you know it's worthwhile? Be open and try it on for

size. If you're having a strong, negative reaction to what's been offered, you may be encountering my good friend resistance. (See more information in Dealing with Doubts and Releasing Resistance on page 197.) You may want to try this very thing you don't want to try. If it feels exciting, go for it. And if it feels off or flat, it probably is. Forget it.

3. **"Random" found good.** The ten-dollar bill on the sidewalk. The entertaining magazine beside you in the airport when there's an hour to wait. The perfect parking space in the perfect place. An article in your Facebook feed that solves a dilemma for you. Good is all around when you're open to it. This will make you laugh. I literally pick up every penny I see on the ground. They are a unit of energy just like any other denomination. And I thank the Universe every single time! What most people have decided is an annoyance, to me is a gift. The more you receive these tiny blessings, the more you'll encounter and realize they aren't so random after all.

4. **Gifts.** They're not just for birthdays. A friend passing on that Instant Pot she never used. Leftovers from your cousin's barbecue. A pick-me-up greeting card exactly when you needed to be uplifted. There are times you are given gifts and you just don't see them as such. Unlike with the not-valuable advice, which can bring in even more, receive this all with love. Even if the Instant Pot was dented or the chicken dry. There is always value to a gift in that someone was thinking of you. Appreciate the gesture even if the gift itself is the "wrong size," metaphorically speaking.

5. **Money, money, money.** If you're employed, don't just collect a paycheck or notice the amount in your account. Consciously receive it. The same goes for money given by friends, tips from customers, or gifts from family. If you're receiving unemployment benefits, consciously receive that too. The temptation can be to look at that amount and focus on it being too low or not what you're used to making. There may even be embarrassment. See this as an area for healing so

you can appreciate every dollar without pain. Print out your checking account statement, and next to every deposit, write, "Thank you, Universe. I gratefully receive this and more."

How to Apply Grace and Appreciation

1. **Allow discomfort.** If receiving brings up discomfort in any form like cringing, minimizing, avoiding, grimacing, or fleeing, then those feelings need to be addressed rather than ignored. Here's how:

   - Set an intention for catching the discomfort.

   - Once you're aware of it, stop and simply be with it. What does the discomfort feel like? Is it rumbling in your stomach? A furrow forming across your brow? Observe it.

   - And breathe in through the nose and out through the mouth. If tempted to shut down, numb out, or get distracted, resist this urge by any means necessary. Pull yourself back and let yourself be with it. Getting comfortable with being uncomfortable will serve your growth in many profound ways. This is a gentle area to get started with it.

2. **Say it.** Speak the grace and appreciation out loud, even if it's just to yourself. Please be sure that it is sincere. Say:

   - *Thank you.*

   - *You're so welcome.*

   - *I really appreciate you saying that, giving me that, noticing that.*

   - *This is just what I needed.*

   - *I can really use this.*

   - *I really appreciate you thinking of me.*

   - *This means so much.*

No need to reinvent the wheel here. Or become a poet laureate. Simple and sincere words shared openly land lovingly.

3. **Ask yourself what, why, and how.**

• What do you appreciate about what you're receiving?

• Why is it meaningful?

• How is it beneficial to you?

> Example:
>
> When my first book hit the market, I received an unexpected tag in a tweet. An editor I long admired of a magazine I had long enjoyed had chosen my book to be featured in a top-ten list. I did not know her personally, had no idea how she learned of the book, and was very pleasantly surprised. In such gratitude and joy, I reached out to thank her and was then invited onto her radio show. One gift became another. Here's how I answered the above questions.

— *What do I appreciate about this?*

> I wrote my book to help people, and it will now reach more people outside of my circle. My publisher will be happy the book is getting good publicity. The conversation with the editor made me feel seen. She so got what I was trying to accomplish with this material. She was kind and generous. I truly enjoyed our conversation.

— *Why is it meaningful?*

> My life's work is being validated by a person I respect. I got to reexperience the passion I feel for healing and share that with others.

— *How was/is it beneficial?*

> I got sweet emails from people who loved the interview and wanted to know more.

4. **Resist the urge to return a gift with a gift.** This often comes from not feeling worthy. If you're tempted to immediately return a compliment with a compliment or a gift for a gift, you are deflecting your receiving. In the discomfort, you are returning to your giving default. Immediate reciprocity is a rule of obligation, not receptivity or generosity. Yes, you will give back to life and make that a part of your practice. But who you give to may not look like the giver standing before you. Let yourself receive first, and acknowledge you are worthy of this and more.

7 Easy Things to Do *Right Now* That Will Attract More Good

1. **Increase tipping.**
   And give the increased tip with sincere appreciation. Because if not now, when?

2. **Clean a closet or drawer.**
   Just start with one and see it through to completion.

3. **Write thank-you notes.**
   Go old-school and use pretty stationery or crisp cards. Be genuine and loving.

4. **Clear your energy.**
   Imagine golden light moving through your body and out into your entire living space.

5. **Get out in nature.**
   A walk in nature is a perfect cure-all.

6. **Dance.**
   Turn up the music and shake your tail feather!

7. **Hum.**
   Close those lips and hold a single note or go with an entire tune.

Manifesting Alchemy Principle 4

GIVE WHAT YOU WANT TO RECEIVE

started with the topic of receiving first because over-giving can be the sign of a person who doesn't have enough. With the circles I run in of spiritual and bighearted people, there is an over-giving epidemic. I've seen people I care about, exhausted, broke people, literally push money and support back as soon as it's offered. And they wonder why they are exhausted and broke!

> No one has ever become poor by giving.
> —**Anne Frank**

Giving and receiving are two parts of a cycle of flow. If you're an over-receiver, you're likely to feel guilty. And under-receivers often feel resentful. Allow the cycle to flow so you're becoming ever increasingly generous with both giving and receiving.

Find ways to give what you most want to receive.

Years ago, I had a series of boyfriends who shunned Valentine's Day. Suddenly, come the beginning of February, they'd get extremely principled. "It's just a made-up Hallmark holiday, Kris. It's just making us be over-consumers!" I heard this, I'm not kidding you, from three different beaus over five years, and they did not know each other. The only thing they had in common was me. And of course, the less anyone wanted to celebrate with me, the more, more, more I wanted it! The card, the candy, the flowers, oh my! Mine, mine, mine!

Choosing to be single for a while, I worked on upgrading my romantic standards. It was time for a different kind of man. When that first solo Valentine's Day approached, I was filled with dread. Rather than drowning in a bottle of wine, I knew I had three choices. Ignore it (not so easy), hate it (too easy!), or turn it around (man, do I like a challenge!) I decided to give what I hadn't been receiving. I chose five single gal pals and made a Valentine's Day I knew they wouldn't forget. I created gorgeous gift baskets filled with goodies. I baked French cookies from an old recipe and, while hot, twisted them into the shape of fortune cookies. I threaded the insides with ribbon inscribed with love quotes from famous authors. A set of champagne glasses were filled with red candies. Books on best screen kisses and true love stories were essential inclusions. And I designed a custom card, letting them know they were special and worthy of so much love. I delivered the baskets to their front doors, ringing their bells, and presenting with a big hug and well wishes. I became jam-packed with so much love, fun, and joy, more than I had ever experienced on a V-Day date. Unexpectedly, Valentine's Day became my favorite holiday. And by the next year, I had a sweetie who made dinner reservations, donned a red shirt, and showered me with love and presents. Nonetheless, I kept my Cupid act going because I absolutely delighted in showering my sweet friends with beauty and light. Once a friend had a life partner, I cut her loose and added another single lady to my roster.

Now, notice I didn't give in ways I didn't want to. Or out of obligation. Or spend money I didn't have. Or decide to do this when I was already giving so much. I gave in ways that felt enriching to me and others, drawing more good into my life. I made this act of giving a fun and creative adventure that uplifted me even more than the recipients.

Giving and receiving are one flow. As I give, so do I receive. And when I receive well, I have that much more to give. Plus, giving makes a declarative statement to yourself and the Universe:

I have more than enough. I am enough. I can give because I know I'll always be supported in return.

This is an act of embodying your enoughness.

5

Manifesting Alchemy Principle 5

MAKING ROOM FOR THE NEW

A classic metaphysical concept I first learned was: the Universe abhors a vacuum.

In other words, the Universe doesn't like unoccupied space. To create a new anything often requires making room so that that new job/lover/trip can come in.

There are times when that vacuum is quite literal. I'm looking for a television so I donate the old one first. Right after, I find the perfect replacement on sale. Now, I don't usually advise people to quit their jobs before they have found a new one. The one exception is if the workplace is compromising their health. Otherwise, in my experience, it's much easier for people to find new work when they're

> Keeping baggage from the past will leave no room for the happiness in the future.
> —**Wayne L. Misner**

currently employed and not terribly worried about money. But there are times the Universe has other plans. This happened with me.

I had left a long and successful career in social services to work for a small, modern company. It was a radical change and one that was long overdue. I went from my own office with a window to working from home, using my own computer, and connecting with fellow employees via Skype. This was a high-pressure, high-stress environment, with almost no training, very little planning, and a lot of moving on your feet, with back-to-back product launches and long hours. Any fantasies I had held about working for a company that taught practices I used and believed in were quickly dispelled. Within a week, I thought, *Oh no, what have I done?* But all the signs were there that this was the right move. And yet, you take yourself with you wherever you go.

> I didn't see it then, but it turned out that getting fired from Apple was the best thing that could have ever happened to me. The heaviness of being successful was replaced by the lightness of being a beginner again, less sure about everything. It freed me to enter one of the most creative periods of my life.
>
> —Steve Jobs

I decided to heal my way through this job. Anytime I felt mistreated, I healed. Anytime I felt undervalued, I healed. Anytime I was given mind-numbing busywork, I healed. I memorized affirmations and repeated them over and over again while I went through the motions. Then I was given a position within the company I truly aspired to and utilized my best skills. I developed a plan. I had already been a part-time energy healer for years. While employed, I would finally buckle down and develop a business plan, newsletter, and social media presence. I hoped to eventually work for the company part-time and do my healing practice the rest of the time, slowly, eventually building my business until I was fully self-employed. I imagined leaving and them wishing me well, proud of what I had accomplished and grateful for my service. *Insert the sound of a needle scratching a record here.* That is *not* how it went down.

A couple of weeks before Christmas, I was let go. It came as an absolute shock. I had been very successful in my new position. How could this have happened? I could hardly move for two days, filled with anger, shame, embarrassment, and despair. What was I going to do now? I cried,

I processed, I stayed up late and slept in like a college student. I went for walks. My life-force battery had been sucked dry by this company and its endless drama. I knew I needed to be recharged.

Within a week, I started my newsletter, learning the program more easily than I had imagined. New clients learned of services and contacted me for sessions. Suddenly, with free time on my hands for the first time in eighteen years, I volunteered to share energy healing practices with any group that would have me. The more I shared, the more client sessions I did, the more deeply I fell in love with my work. My business grew.

Within two months, I realized I would never work for anyone else ever again. I had had a true epiphany. That day, I had agreed to share EFT, an energy healing technique, with a group of mothers in Dobbs Ferry, New York, about an hour from my home. I woke up early to find a bitterly cold February morning. This was a free gig and would be costing me time, gas, tolls. Why the heck had I agreed to this? But my mood shifted the second I began to drive. Snow had blanketed the landscape for months, and it was one of those hyper-bright sunny days. The brilliant sun sparkled across the ice, inviting new possibility. I instantly connected with the women in the group, giving them a mini workshop with handouts and demos. It was supposed to be an hour, but no one wanted to leave, including me.

Afterwards I checked out the downtown, treated myself to a green juice, and headed to nearby Sleepy Hollow for lunch at my favorite Indian restaurant. I was filled with bliss. Before heading home, I visited the waterfronts along the Hudson River, taking pictures of the massive chunks of ice floating there. On the drive back, I had a sudden realization of the date. My former employer was in the middle of another hectic launch. If I had still been employed there, I never would have had this day. I'd have logged on, beginning work at 6:30 a.m., answering emails and putting out fires, choking down food on short breaks, logging out at 10:00 p.m., numbing out to TV for a bit, then falling into bed, only to do that over and over again. I knew I'd never have to do that again. I felt my heart center open, flooding my body with love and gratitude. My days were now my own to spend as I chose. I could now choose to spend them doing what I loved, connecting with incredible people and sharing a gospel of hope, healing, and happiness.

A heaviness rapidly left me. I knew that this was exactly how it had to be. I released the anger, neutralized the shame, and forgave my former "oppressors." I realized that there are times when your light is so big, it outgrows where you are. Getting brutally honest with myself, I knew that as long as I remained employed there, I would have never had the time, energy, and motivation to build my business. The Universe kicked me out of the nest. I didn't want to be kicked out. This was not my well-laid plan. It hurt! I was quite self-righteous about it. I blamed the foot. I got a bunch of bruises from trying to grasp for stray branches on the way down. I worried what people were saying about me as I was falling. And then, the most unexpected miracle happened: I flew.

As I'm writing this, it's been five and a half years since I was let out of that cage. In that time, I've traveled to places I've always wanted to see; spoken in front of hundreds of people, at times ending in standing ovations; taught workshops nationally and internationally; made many new friends; built a successful practice helping thousands of people, along with an outstanding newsletter featuring my original writing and photography; written a book for a very prestigious publisher, recorded its audio, with book number two now sitting in your hands. My time, my energy, my devotion, my focus are all my own. None of this would have happened had I been allowed to remain there.

I am making it!

During this journey, the funniest thing happened. When I was getting a paycheck, I constantly worried about money, about not having enough, about needing to be employed by others to support myself. Now the Universe is my employer, and I hardly ever worry at all. Money flows in and money flows out. When I need it, it shows up, always right on time, and often in surprising ways. When money flows out to bills, expenses, donations, I bless the recipients and know there's more available. When I need time to write, research, travel, or recharge, business will temporarily dry up, giving me time and energy to do what I most need. Yet my needs are always covered.

The Universe decided I was ready way before I did. It created a vacuum in my life that was filled with my soul's purpose. In my shock, embarrassment, and fear, I could not have seen that. It was only in processing my feelings and holding that there was good, somehow, some way, in this change, before it was visible or conscious, that I was able to have that perfect day. I was able to recognize that everything I had experienced had happened exactly the way it needed to. That all of it was perfect.

If you don't create a vacuum, one may be created for you. In my experience, the one you create is always gentler than the one that appears to be out of your control.

Clear Vacuum Examples

1. **Clothing.** If you have a closetful of old, outdated, ill-fitting clothes, donate them. Everyone I've ever advised to do this has quickly found much more attractive replacements, often on sale!

2. **Travel.** You want to go on a particular trip but currently don't have the resources. Put it on the calendar anyway, even if it's two years away. Think of the perfect time to go and label it as "My trip to Paris." Send an email to human resources requesting that time off. Tell friends, "I'm going on vacation the second week in July." Don't tell them you're creating a vacuum so you can manifest a trip to Paris. Just allow them to share in your excitement about going away. Make the space for it to happen.

3. **Household Items.** That damn refrigerator that always freezes your spring mix? You can never seem to find anything in it! Start researching where you can donate it or how to properly dispose of it in your town. Ask around if anyone needs a free fridge. Eat out of the freezer to reduce the work of a changeover. Clean it out and get rid of that old German mustard you bought for a 2012 Oktoberfest. Prepare space for a new one.

"I Don't Know What This Has to Do with That" Vacuums

Clear clutter. Clean out a closet. Peruse the filing cabinet and get shredding. Get real. You're never going to use that panini press. Give it to someone who will. That old painting from your grandmother that everyone says is a valuable family heirloom but makes you cringe every time you walk past it? Sell it or give it to someone else in the family. If you need a financial boost, start here. Clutter clogs up energetic flow, preventing the new from coming in, including cash. One of the most effective money manifesting practices starts with doing this.

Clearing Clutter

1. **Mentally review your home.** Evaluate every room, hallway, and closet, the attic, the basement, and the garage. Which areas contain clutter? Write it all down. Include storage on your devices too!

2. **For each area, detail the nature of the clutter (unfiled papers, stacks of kids' homework, unused jewelry, old clothes, etc.).**

3. **Write a plan to remove this clutter.** Find places to donate or friends to give to.

4. **Do you need help?** Write names of people you know who may be willing to help or professionals to be hired. Consider a trade. A friend helps you and then you help them. If you don't know anyone, affirm, "I attract the right and perfect help in creating a healthy, organized, and serene home."

QUICK BIT ALCHEMY LIST

My 9 Favorite Words for Describing a Rich Life . . . in the Affirmative!

1. I am . . . Flourishing
2. I am . . . Thriving
3. I am . . . Free
4. Life is . . . Luxurious
5. Life is . . . Exquisite
6. Life is . . . Opulent
7. The Universe is . . . Abundant
8. The Universe is . . . Prosperous
9. The Universe is . . . Prolific

Manifesting Alchemy Principle 6

THERE'S WHAT YOU WANT AND WHAT THE UNIVERSE WANTS FOR YOU

Not all desires are created equal.

You're actively working the manifestation process. And it either isn't working, or it worked and the results didn't feel the way you thought they would. If so, it's not the Universe, but the desire that could be off.

There are times when what we want to manifest isn't actually what we desire at all. We just don't know it. It can be what our mothers told us we wanted. Or our churches. Or society at large.

There are times when I'm working with a client and it is just so clear.

Janet came to see me because of her unhappiness with her job. She held a high-level position in a cutting-edge marketing company. The creativity and innovation inspired her. The competitiveness and backstabbing, even within her own department, not so much. The salary was excellent, but the work travel wasn't enjoyable. She could not figure out how to be happy there. The pros clearly outweighed the cons, but it was getting harder and harder to get out of bed in the morning. Every day, she affirmed happiness and joy, focused on her gratitude, but it still eluded her. She blamed herself. There were so many who would love this job. Why didn't she just toughen up already? Janet was sensitive and bighearted. She couldn't understand why everyone wasn't working together for the good of the projects. It was clear to me; this was simply not the right environment for her. For a certain type of person, the high pressure and competition would invigorate and elevate them. Not for someone like Janet. Feeling targeted and unsafe, her creativity shrank and took her joy with it.

> Being human means you will make mistakes. And you will make mistakes, because failure is God's way of moving you in another direction.
>
> —Oprah Winfrey

Janet could have spent the next ten years imagining this job as the dream job, and it would not have changed. The job was out of alignment with her temperament and needs. She could have kept telling herself, *No, this is it. This is the place for me. I'm going to be happy here no matter what!*

As a person genetically predisposed to stubbornness, I know this story well. I can't tell you the number of times I tried to make something be what I wanted and needed it to be where clearly it could not. It's like trying to grow a pine tree in the desert. Wrong conditions!

When I worked in social services, there came a time with no more growth. No more promotions. No advancement at all. Even though I was hardworking, dedicated, and really effective at my job. Even though I was affirming more money and an upper-management position. I could not figure out why what I wanted wasn't happening. One night, I was rereading an essay by Ralph Waldo Emerson and came across a passage that left me stunned. He essentially said, no matter how hard you work, if you're in the wrong place, you will not succeed. I felt like an anvil had been dropped on my head! A little spiritual tough love from 170 years before.

Why did Janet hold on for so long? It paid well. She'd invested eighteen years. Her parents were proud of her. She felt honored to reply when anyone asked what she did for a living. After all, she was nearing forty. How could she change careers now? What would she say at the next high school reunion?

Unfortunately, the Universe and your soul don't care about any of that. They've been around a lot longer than 401(k)s.

When your desires are in alignment with what your soul came to do, manifestation unfolds easily. When they are not, either it doesn't happen or the results feel flat and unsatisfying.

There are times you're simply thinking too small. You've narrowed your desires down by what you believe you are worth. Once your worth has grown, your desire will get a much-needed upgrade, and then *boom*, it materializes.

There are times you're thinking too big. Let me be clear, there is no goal too big it can't be achieved. It can just be too big for now. With huge, audacious goals, there are often steps in between, smaller milestones to achieve. No one goes directly from the mail room to CEO. And TMZ is riddled with horror stories of what happens to people who got famous overnight. You've got some growing and learning to do. That growth prepares you for the ultimate end result you're seeking. Break it down into bite-size pieces so you don't choke.

And there are times when what you're trying to create is completely off the mark. You can expend your energy creating someone else's perfect life. Even if you make it happen, it will not satisfy you.

Janet began volunteering in a local community arts program for teens. Her creativity came back to life, and she often took her demonstration projects home to finish them. More and more, she looked forward to being with those kids and their wide-eyed wonder, sarcastic jokes, and high energy. It came so naturally. Within a few months, she learned the CEO was retiring and found herself saying, "I'd love to submit." Her experience in the marketing world was very attractive to the board, who wanted to expand services and needed increased grant funding and visibility. She got the job! And she was terrified! She had never been a CEO or worked in the nonprofit world, yet she couldn't deny it, this just felt right. She lost about 15 percent of her income but gained fifteen to twenty hours more free time per week, time she spent on her own art, which began selling. Within two years, she was making more than she ever had. Sleeping better and feeling more at ease allowed her high blood pressure to go away for good.

> Two things I'm trying to work on are openness and flexibility.
> —Lili Taylor

Declare what you want but be open to inspiration along the way. The Universe knows you better than you know yourself and will have exciting ideas for you.

It's all part of the creative experimentation.

Declare what you want.

Release attachment.

Expect good.

Be open.

Receive graciously.

7

Manifesting Alchemy Principle 7

SURRENDER AND CONTROL

M anifestation is a dance between control and surrender. There's what you are able to control. Your thoughts and feelings. Getting clear about what you want. Developing habits that serve your dreams. Forgiving yourself, the Universe, and others. This requires conscious control. Thoughts that are allowed to go unchecked can very easily make wrong assumptions and take you on a bumpy ride. Feelings that are stifled and remain unprocessed will rise up, often at the worst possible times. You are responsible for you. Let your inner control freak know that this is their job.

> The moment of surrender is not when life is over, it's when it begins.
> —Marianne Williamson

And then there's surrender.

Normally, the word *surrender* brings up an image of giving up. Waving the white flag. Throwing in the towel. At the end of your rope. The last straw. Feel free to fill in another cliché of your choice here too!

No wonder we are distrustful of this practice. Nobody likes a quitter after all.

What if I told you that surrender was the key to having more of what you want? That's right. You've gotten clear, released the blocks, and done the work. You're looking for the good in life and seeing more of it than you have before. You've navigated the bumps and gotten back on track. And listened for intuitive insights and acted on them. You've done your part. Now: Let. It. Go.

Surrender is not giving up; it's giving over to that which is greater than yourself. It's what's made the biggest difference for every successful person you've ever admired. That which has kept the twelve-step member sober. That which has launched millions of ideas and creations.

There's what's yours to do.

And then there's the Universe's work.

When you're clear about this, you won't get overwhelmed on those tasks that are simply not yours.

The Universe creates divine order with timing, locations, opportunities, the right people, and the ideal convergence of these elements.

Surrender requires trust. And whether you and the Universe are new friends or coming back together after a breakup, that can be frightening. How do you trust that which is seemingly invisible? Or just a force you do not know yet. Or what if you feel you've been let down or were not protected or even punished in a painful way?

MANIFESTING MINI PROCESS

Clearing the Air with the Universe Ritual

Now's the time to air your grievances with the Universe. Here's something you may not know. The Universe can take it. No matter how resentful or angry you may be. There is nothing It cannot handle.

Start by creating a list of every time you felt let down by the Universe (or God).

Give each memory a title. Write a few sentences about what went wrong and how it made you feel. Include old ideas you had about the Universe that were confusing or upsetting.

Now stand up and let the Universe have it! Yell, shout, blame, demand, say, "Enough is enough." Stamp your feet. Yell, "It's not fair!"

Now imagine a large box in front of you. Breathe in and exhale the memory titles into the box. If any pictures or symbols come up, throw those in the box too. Now close the lid and visualize handing it over to the Universe. It could look like plopping it in a large set of hands or a giant ball of light, or into something that looks like a star. Breathe in and exhale, letting it go.

Say, "I release this over to you, Universe. I'm done. Help me retain whatever lessons I needed to learn. Encode them in my cells. Dissolve the pain and set me free. I fully and freely give this to you completely here and now."

If emotion comes up, allow it to flow and imagine it also going to the Universe. Tears are our built-in release valve. Let them flow. Use the breath to move them through and out of you.

Now say, "Universe, I'm willing to have a new relationship with you. I'm willing to work together on my dreams. I'm willing to see you clearly now. Transform me into one who is able to trust. Every day, show me that you are loving, protecting, and guiding me. Show me that I can trust you with my biggest goals. Show me the way."

> Try something different—surrender.
> —Rumi

Purchase something to symbolize a new beginning and fresh start with the Universe. Perhaps flowers or a new plant or a piece of jewelry.

There are times this exercise may need to be repeated. Like if a new disappointment arises, for example. But not always. Don't underestimate what this ritual can do. I've had countless students return to me with absolute relief. Relief that they won't be punished for being mad at their Higher Power. Relief that they can take a stand for themselves. Relief that they can develop a new relationship with the Universe based on their current understandings. And relief that the most difficult parts of manifestation they get to hand over!

Here's the Universe's job:

- Align all the correct elements.

- Work through people, circumstances, minds, bodies,

everything that needs to shift for this manifestation to happen.

- Set perfect timing.

- Bring about the "how."

Whenever you're caught up in wondering about the above, you now know:

This isn't your job. This is the Universe's job. Give it out and go back to your tasks. Or set it and forget it. Your part may indeed be complete. Let it go and focus on feeling fun and joy in the present.

PART TWO

The 9 Powerful Manifesting Alchemy Practices

Introduction to Practices: Manifesting Alchemy—What to Keep in Mind

It's important to remember on this journey: you are more than just a mind. With much of old-school metaphysics, and let's face it, with some modern teachings as well, the focus is only on thoughts.

"Change your thinking, change your life."

"Your thoughts create things."

"What you're living today was what you were thinking yesterday."

I will certainly be asking you to look at what you spend much of your mental energy on. Changing your thinking does indeed change your life. Most of us are caught in endless loops, repeating the same thought patterns over and over again. Have you ever spoken to a good friend about something they just can't seem to let go? Like, for example, their cheating louse of an ex-husband? Once he's entered the topic of conversation, you can almost repeat word for word what your friend is saying. You've heard it a thousand times before. And here she goes again. It's like there's a recording in her forehead. His name hits the Play button. Often, loops are the narration of experiences where we've felt let down: by a person, an organization, or by life itself. It was so unfair! Anyplace where you've felt victimized and not vindicated will show up as blocks to be healed. That healing can take place on the mental level of creation. Or it may require one or more of the other levels.

In addition to practices that work on the mental level of creation, I'm going to introduce others that work with emotional, physical, and energetic levels of creation. There are some manifestations, and blocks to achieving them, that benefit from being approached by a different angle. This gives you several options to try, testing what works best for you and what doesn't.

Temperament

I believe a factor in what practices work and don't work as well can be related to individual temperament. Each of us is born with a personality and a temperament, or a tendency for certain moods. Caregivers of children all know this. And while we are all tremendously shaped by the families, cultures, religions (or no religion), and communities we are born into, there are unchangeable parts of us that arrived at conception. The nature-versus-nurture debate is fascinating. Studies of identical twins separated at birth and raised in very different households showed researchers what they weren't expecting: that children aren't total blank slates after all. I have seen this in my own life. I have changed in so many profound ways over the past thirty years. When I had social anxiety, speaking to a stranger was unthinkable. It was hard enough to talk with people I knew! Now I can chat with my seatmate on a plane or introduce myself to a person at a conference quite easily. Not to forget standing on a stage speaking to hundreds of people! Social anxiety was not my natural temperament but a healable condition. If I had decided I was just shy, I may not have realized this could change. Yet I am still very much an introvert. I have moments of being extroverted, like when I'm throwing a raucous Halloween party. The wild reveler is summoned from within me. But on an average night, you won't find me in a large group at a bar. I prefer one-on-one conversations and quiet time for reading, creative projects, and spiritual practices. That's my normal temperament.

You may be a big thinker. If you've ever spent hours online researching the right rental car company or the history behind the *Hindenburg* disaster, that may be you. Using the mental level processes may feel more comfortable and yield better results.

If you're a compassionate, bighearted sensitive, mental level processes may fall flat and even feel meaningless to you. For you, the feeling nature of your desires will make the manifestation process easy and even joyous.

Process Levels of Creation

Mental Level
Changing with thoughts to carve new neural pathways

Emotional Level
Evoking specific feeling states

Physical Level
Using movement to embody a desired creation

Energetic Level
Working with the body's natural energy field to create a new state of being

All these levels approach creation from different angles. Find the angle that works best for you.

Throughout this book, you will be given assignments to harness the energy of life and make your dreams a reality. In many instances, you will have options. If one process isn't arousing your enthusiasm, check out another level practice and feel free to use it instead. It's important to make the manifestation process enjoyable and fun. The more you enjoy these practices, the better you will feel, and the more likely you will be to make them a part of your life. You may begin manifesting with one specific goal in mind, that once achieved, you will put this kind of work aside. That is a valid approach, and regularly integrating these practices into your life will move every aspect forward in the most extraordinary ways.

8

Manifesting Alchemy Practice 1

AFFIRMATIONS AND SCRIPTING

Affirmations

Affirmations are statements of spiritual truth, not (yet) factual truth. You are affirming what you'd like to believe, feel, or have. Affirmations are stated in the present tense, as if this is what you're already experiencing. Affirmations program the subconscious mind. When practiced regularly, they can delete previous mental ideas that are in opposition to what you'd like to create.

Affirmations can be secular in nature or spiritual. You can experiment and see which alleviate stress and give you a positive boost.

> Take care what words you speak that follow "I am." In so speaking you create your life.
>
> —**Alan Cohen**

How to Create Them

Begin with the end results in mind.

What do you want? How do you want to feel? What would you say if you were experiencing this now?

Beginning with "I am" is always a powerful place to start.

Specific Affirmations

These are crafted to your specific circumstances, often to address a current problem.

Examples:

I have more than enough money to repair the car and pay for an Uber.

I am confidently and competently leading this meeting.

My rent is easily paid in full each month.

The Universe brings me my ideal mate now.

General Affirmations

These affirm general good circumstances, feelings, and well-being.

Examples:

Everything is going my way.

I was born under a lucky star.

My life is blessed, and I am content.

The Universe is providing everything I need.

What if affirmations feel completely unbelievable?

That's normally how they start. If they were already believable, you wouldn't need to say them.

1. **Repetition not only makes them believable, it makes them manifest.** Repeat as often as possible.

2. **You can start by recrafting them using phrases like, "I am willing." "I'd like to believe." "I'm willing to be open to the Universe providing everything I need." "I'd like to believe the Universe is providing everything I need."** Once your willingness or believability grows and your resistance reduces, you can go direct to the outcome you'd like to experience.

How to Use Them

1. **Repeat them mentally.** Ideally, you'd like affirmations to be short and simple enough that they can be easily memorized. Stick with one or two related to the same area of growth. Repeat them over and over again, especially during times of waiting and boredom:

   - On your commute

   - While stopped at a red light

   - In the shower

   - As soon as you wake up and just before you go to sleep

   - In line at a store

   - While walking or doing other forms of exercise

   - While cleaning

   - In an unimportant meeting

   Work them into your everyday routine so they become a positive habit.

2. **State them out loud.** In many of the above situations, you can state them out loud. Many believe that speaking them out loud in our own voice reinforces this new truth to the subconscious, packing a powerful programming punch.

3. **Write them down.** Again, repetition is key. In your notebook, write your affirmations over and over again. It may make you feel like Bart Simpson. Each episode opening, he takes his punishment and writes over and over on the chalkboard what he will no longer do. Remember: this is not a punishment. Make it fun. Put on either wordless or uplifting music.

4. **Place them under your pillow.** Write the affirmations, read them, then place them under your pillow each night. Reread in the morning.

5. **Display them (make them visual & visible).** Print out or write multiple copies and place them everywhere. Your bathroom mirror, in your car, on kitchen cabinets, on the TV remote. But don't just leave them there. Use them. Each time you see them, repeat them.

> The imagination is the golden pathway to everywhere.
>
> **—Terence McKenna**

6. **Sing them.** I'm definitely not a song-writer, but I created a little ditty when I was having trouble leaving for the office on time. In hindsight, perhaps I should have affirmed having plenty of time! Instead, I focused on a smooth and speedy commute.

   Green lights, nothing but green lights,
   Green lights, wherever I go,
   Green lights, I'm seeing those green lights,
   Green lights, allow me to flow.

7. **Record them and play the audio while sleeping.** As a light sleeper, this one never worked for me. But I have colleagues who have used this process with great success. Your conscious mind is out of the way. The subconscious, however, never shuts down. This is its busy time, working out stresses in your dreams. As a fertile time period, listening to affirmations while sleeping allows them to easily take root.

   Record a voice memo on your smartphone. Record yourself saying the affirmation(s). Put some gusto into it. Play on repeat as you're sleeping.

8. **Use them with other practices included in this book.** Throughout the book, you will see affirmations used in a myriad of ways. In most places, I offer examples. I'm also encouraging you to make your own, using your own voice and lingo, with words that have meaning for you. The more meaningful and real they feel for you, the better the impact.

Scripting

As humans, storytelling is one of our most valuable tools for sharing information and lessons. It's how information was shared for centuries. Normally, we tell a story after it has occurred. Here's the setting, then the narrative, and a conclusion.

Scripting is writing a story, as you would like it to unfold, before it has happened. This works particularly well for events.

My student Johan was feeling chewed up by the audition process. A talented actor nearing his forties, he was beginning to lose hope that he'd ever be able to support himself doing what he loved most. Every audition seemed to go the same. He spent time analyzing and preparing, nervous about doing his best. He would show up early, looking the part, and attempt to please the casting agents. The last dozen auditions ended exactly the same way. He was told he simply missed the mark for what they had in mind. Now these were twelve completely dissimilar projects with different staff. The only thing they had in common was Johan.

> There is no greater agony than bearing an untold story inside you.
> —Maya Angelou

Since he was a person comfortable with scripts, I encouraged him to outline his next audition in advance.

I asked him: What is the best that can happen here? And how do you want to feel?

His answers were:

- I want to feel at ease with the process. Actually, I'd like to not care whether I get it or not. To somehow be unattached to what happens.

- I'd like to approach the character from what I feel is the best angle, rather than try to guess what they're looking for. After all, experience has shown I'm terrible at it!

- I want to enjoy the process. Enjoy meeting them instead of being afraid of them. To be playful about it all.

- I don't want them to reject me openly. If they don't want me, they can send an email!

I had him craft this into an affirmative, present tense, script.

My Audition

I am excited about this project and the potential opportunity. All nerves disappear as I drive to the audition site. I trust that if this project is right for me, it will work out. I check in but hardly notice the other actors and instead focus on the script. I allow the character to come alive within me. I remember why I love this work. The casting agents are friendly, open, and welcoming. I launch into my performance, easily hitting all the marks. They give me their full attention and respect. I leave feeling valued and seen. I love to audition!

The next audition unfolded almost exactly as he'd scripted. A bonus experience is that he saw an old friend from acting class at the audition who gave him a tip on another project he thought Johan would be perfect for. He didn't get the first role. But the one his friend recommended resulted in his first role in a television pilot. Johan tossed aside his waiter aprons for good and is now a working actor.

Trust that little voice in your head that says, "Wouldn't it be interesting if . . ." and then do it.

—Duane Michals

9

Manifesting Alchemy Practice 2

PRAYERS AND AFFIRMATIVE INTENTIONS

f you weren't raised in a praying family, the idea of doing this may feel confusing, overwhelming, or downright ridiculous. "How can this do anything?" many have said to me. If you were raised in a praying family and didn't find value in it, you may feel much the same. I want you to know I was quite the prayer skeptic myself. Most kids have invisible friends. For me, those friends were deities. Talking to God and any invisible presence who could listen or be helpful felt comforting, so that's what I naturally did. But the trusting, innocent child in me grew into a bitter and cynical young adult who had seen her fill of heartache and struggle. It was then quite surprising to me that during a particularly painful time period of my life, I once again turned to prayer, and it ushered in huge changes for me. Be open to trying prayer (again) and see what it can do in your life.

> Prayer is powerful. It can heal, prayer can give, and it can change lives.
>
> —Shane DeCreshio

When to Pray

Anytime! I normally begin and end my day with prayer. I also get prayer requests from others, which can arrive from around the world, at all times daily. Therefore, I set aside time for those as well. I also say little ones throughout my day. And there are times I simply talk to the Universe, usually when I'm driving. I give updates, share how I'm feeling and what I'm dreaming about. Like a divine board meeting.

How to Pray

Don't overthink. *Just do it.* There are times I relax and get into a meditative state. There are times I pray while panicked. Let go of any right or wrong, and just allow. The more you do it, the more you will see what works best for you.

I've included prayer examples here for you to try. And I encourage you to tweak these or make up your own, either using mine as a format or going rogue and just talking to the Universe.

Asking Prayers

Prayers to Prepare for a Best Life

Dearest Universe, prepare me for a life with more love, abundance, happiness, and joy. Create the perfect conditions so I can receive easily. Open everything that needs to be opened. Help me feel secure as I grow. Thank you for this. Amen.

Sweet Universe, prepare every level and dimension of my being to create with You my highest and best life. I welcome all Your love and support. May this be so.

Prayer to Trust

All Powerful Universe, teach me how to trust in You and to know that all I need is being provided in divine timing. Help me relax, let go, and trust all is well and that I am safe and loved. Amen.

Prayer for High Self-Esteem / Deservability

Universe, dissolve all mistaken past ideas about myself and show me how I am a perfect piece of You. Raise my standards. Show me that I'm worthy of a very good life in every way. Thank You, for everything. Amen.

Prayer to Be a Good Receiver

Universe, make me an open vessel who easily receives all Your good. Whatever I need to do to receive generously, show me how to do this. Remind me that as I receive, so shall I give. Grateful for this, I give over to You.

Prayer for Abundance

Universe, I know this is an abundant world. Please show this abundance to me and make it manifest in every area of my life. Open up Your luxurious bounty and let it rain into my consciousness and experiences. Thank You for always hearing me. I let this go and let it be so.

Prayers for Good Health

Oh, Universe, change my body into one that is happy, is healthy, and glows with beauty and vitality. Unfurl perfect balance and harmony in every cell and remind me that I am whole. Shall this be so now.

Almighty Universe, I give this health condition and all my feelings about it over to You, totally and completely. Show me the way back to vibrant well-being now. Thank You for loving me and for taking this burden from me.

Affirmative Prayers

> When prayer removes distrust and doubt and enters the field of mental certainty, it becomes faith.
>
> **—Ernest Holmes**

Here is a layout of an affirmative prayer, also called Spiritual Mind Treatment, which was created by mystic Ernest Holmes and featured in the metaphysical classic tome *The Science of Mind*. This type of prayer is a proven method for manifestation. You acknowledge the powers of the Universe, your connection to It, affirm your desires as happening, give thanks for this happening now, and let it go.

The middle section is for what you're seeking to manifest. Under the basic layout, I give options for that section. Choose what works best for your needs and simply insert it in between the opening and closing.

Opening

"I know there is only one power and one force that has created everything that exists. I know this power as the Universe. The Universe is both the creator and the creation. The Universe is all knowing and all powerful. The Universe is everywhere present, including within me and all levels of my being. It can only be this way. There is no separation. When I think this, when I say this, I unleash an inner knowing and I remember . . ."

Closing

"I express abundant gratitude for this divine manifestation now. I gracefully receive and appreciate it with all my heart. Thank you, Universe, for this good. I now surrender, let go into the only moment there is, and that moment is now, and trust that this is already perfectly done. And so it is."

Affirmative Intentions by Topic

I've included examples for affirmative intentions here.

Money/Abundance

The Universe dissolves all ideas of lack. My life is filled with overflowing abundance. I have more than enough money to pay for all expenses, desires, savings, and to share. I relax knowing I am prospered in every way. I am worthy of all this good and so much more.

Employment

I am working at the perfect place for me! This job uses my skills, talents, and gifts and gives me room to grow. I work with and for

When life itself has become a prayer, we are connected to that source of love and life.
—Brian Hardin

people I really like and respect, and they like and respect me too. I enjoy every aspect, including the lavish pay.

Health

Every place of unease in my body melts permanently away now. I am filled with the life force of the Universe! I live and move with exuberant energy, flexibility, and strength. All my systems of the body work perfectly and in harmony with one another.

Self-Love

The Universe within and all around me loves me unconditionally. Anything in opposition to this is released from my being. There is only love. I choose to love and accept all parts of myself, that which I like and approve of, and everything else too! I am a beloved child of this infinite essence of life and worthy of all love, including my own. I give that to myself generously now.

Good Travel

Every aspect of this trip is in the Universe's hands. All travel is safe, comfortable, and right on time. Anything I need to know, I know. Anything I need to see, I see. Anyone I need to meet, I meet. I experience great joy and satisfaction as this visit unfolds in divine order. I am filled with awe, wonder, and grace as I soak up this beautiful piece of the world.

Friendships/Community

I have found my tribe. I am surrounded by like-minded, trustworthy, loving people who reflect my deepest beliefs and values. I enjoy our social times together where we share laughter, fun, and enriching conversations. I appreciate how we show up for and support one another generously. I am so happy being seen, known, and loved.

Romantic Relationship / Ideal Mate

I am attracting the right and perfect life partner into my world. We meet at the right time and in the perfect way, recognizing in one another that there's a sacred connection between us. We connect mentally. We love to talk to each other. We connect emotionally. We provide love, tenderness, compassion, and understanding to one another, feeling a true heart link. We connect physically. We are wildly attracted to one another! And we connect spiritually. My mate feels like home to me and I to them. We both give to one another and receive from one another joyously. We are joined together to celebrate our love and the Universe.

———————

Making prayer a part of your manifestation journey ensures you are never alone and have the greatest support possible!

10

Manifesting Alchemy Practice 3

INSPIRED ACTION AND ASKING FOR SIGNS

Inspired Action and Asking for Signs

On the path to manifestation, you will need to act. Ideally, it will be inspired action. That means you forge the path in consciousness first, on the invisible plain that is within your energy field. You get clear, imagine, daydream, foster the feelings, dissolve the blocks, embody the vision, and surrender. Then you get impulses, ideas, inspirations, and motivations to take specific actions. When these arise, act on them, and do so immediately.

> Remember the quiet wonders. The world has more need of them than it has for warriors.
>
> —**Charles de Lint**

Have you ever looked for a job and sent out dozens of résumés, only to get almost no response? That is an investment that didn't yield a worthwhile return. Conventional wisdom says to send as many as possible. Cast a wide net.

Knock on a thousand doors. There may be times on the journey where you need to persevere. But scattering your energy will not pay off.

Inspired action is so powerful because you make moves that create results. This saves time, energy, money, and motivation. You get an instinct, a thought, an idea, to visit a particular website, read a specific book, email an old friend or business associate. And that action leads to the next step toward achieving your goal. When this unfolds, act immediately!

Here are a few examples from my students:

Carla was consciously creating a divine love relationship. She hadn't dated anyone since her bitter divorce five years before. The divorce had given her a lot of evidence about what she did not want in a long-term mate. She spent time cleaning up the past, and this revealed a new hopefulness about finding love. From that hope, she began to imagine deep conversations, Sunday morning snuggle-fests, and a much-desired trip to New Zealand, zip-lining hand in hand with her man. While she was cultivating the thoughts and feelings of true love, she held off on dating apps and actively pursuing potentials at gatherings, despite the urging of her friends. It just didn't feel quite right. Then her high school childhood buddy Steve tracked her down on Facebook. One night, they spoke for hours, catching up on all the highlights and lowlights over the past thirty years. It felt synchronistic that they were back in touch after all these years! Carla mentioned she was thinking of learning to sell real estate, and Steve suggested she contact the agent he had recently hired. Tony not only sold real estate but trained new agents. He might be able to advise her on how to learn the trade and get started. Even though she wasn't sure if she was ready to begin this venture, calling Tony felt like the correct action to take. Normally, Carla wasn't comfortable contacting people she didn't already know, but she found herself calling anyway. From the moment she spoke with him, he seemed familiar, kind, and knowledgeable. She immediately felt at ease. They developed a friendship as he suggested courses to take and pitfalls to be aware of. Within two months, they began dating and married within a year. Everything had fallen, seemingly miraculously, into place.

Calling Tony was inspired action. It wasn't even an action that appeared to be about love. But it was a suggestion that felt easy, comfortable, and right. Carla somehow knew that the man for her wasn't to be found online or in her immediate circle. She waited until an inspired move appeared and acted on it. Her old friend Steve was the conduit. Later, she asked him why he had tracked her down at that time. Steve said he had watched a documentary on roller-skating, and, remembering it was her favorite high school activity, he felt inspired to locate her. So it was actually two inspired actions that brought Carla and Tony together.

Omar came to my class begrudgingly. His boyfriend, my client Patrick, had gently suggested, then later pushed him to come. Omar absolutely detested his job as an accountant for a prestigious law firm. Patrick simply could no longer tolerate the daily complaining. An ultimatum was drawn. Omar would either take my class or no longer whine about the job. He didn't necessarily believe in this stuff, but he admitted that Patrick's life had changed in huge ways upon becoming a manifestor. Omar learned he did enjoy numbers and budgets; they had always come easily to him. It was the environment that felt crushing. Formal suits, endless meetings, aggressive colleagues, and constant "imperative" demands, even on weekends. He was too exhausted to even update his résumé, let alone look for another job. And how could he possibly leave the large salary and perks? I advised him to mentally put the job aside for now. To show up, go through the motions, but with a sense of detachment. I helped him release some fears of shutting off the work emails on weekends. Much to his surprise, there weren't any repercussions from his setting boundaries that he couldn't handle. He got clear about what he wanted his ideal work life to look like: fewer hours, an easier commute, a softer and more socially conscious company vibe, colleagues with a sense of humor, and casual attire. He also was certain about how he wanted to feel: valued, respected, relaxed, and jovial. Before my course ended, he got a message on LinkedIn from a former colleague. He had left the law firm in a huff over five years before and Omar was surprised he even remembered him. Rowan was now a lawyer for a large tech firm, and they were looking for an accountant with Omar's qualifications. With a new energy to move forward, he updated his résumé and sent it immediately. The interview took place in a playful loft space with beanbag chairs, a soda fountain, and foosball table! He was greeted warmly by comfortably dressed employees who shared the company's many benefits, like paid time off for volunteering for a cause of his choice, tropical brainstorming retreats, and an emphasis on proper work-life balance. The CEO had been a member of the same college fraternity. They had instant rapport. He got the job and, along with it, a 10 percent bump in salary and fifteen-minute-shorter commute. A year later, impressed with the supportive corporate culture, Patrick joined the team as a graphic designer.

As long as Omar was exhausted and stuck in negativity, it would have been very difficult to find any new job, let alone the right job. Once he set boundaries, cleared fear, and created a vision for what could be, a divine opportunity presented itself, and he was then prepared to act on it.

In these two previous examples, the Universe worked through people my students had previously known, who provided outlets for manifestation. Here's a different example of inspired action.

Kelly had been a talented painter since childhood. Her mother always bragged, "You drew before you walked!" After having her third child, balancing motherhood with her full-time job meant putting art aside, for a year or two, or such was the plan. Now thirteen years had gone by since she'd picked up a brush. She wanted to begin again, but each time she sat down at her easel, she felt rusty and uninspired. When starting to manifest, her dream was to have her work hang in a gallery. After forgiving herself for such a long creative absence, she knew she wanted to feel inspired, passionate, and filled with a zest for life. One of her friends mentioned attending a brilliant off-Broadway musical based on the artist van Gogh. It didn't catch Kelly's attention. Then another friend had returned from a trip to Holland and regaled her with how moved she had been by the Van Gogh Museum. *Eh,* Kelly thought. She had never been a fan. Her middle child spoke of learning about the artist in school. Still, nothing. Then while browsing her favorite bookstore, she felt drawn to a calendar featuring van Gogh's works. It being February, the calendar was 75 percent off. She told herself her son might enjoy the pictures. Two nights after purchasing it, she woke up in the middle of the night and could not get back to sleep. She found herself browsing through the calendar. It was like she was seeing his works for the first time. Pulling out a sketch pad, she began to draw with a sweeping flow she hadn't experienced before. By morning, she was painting, and in a unique style that captivated her. Two years later, she had her very first gallery showing.

Kelly kept getting signs that an artist long gone was the key to finding new innovative flow. Due to van Gogh's popularity and her previous exposure to his work, she had dismissed the hints that kept presenting themselves to her until inspired action drew her to the calendar that opened everything for her.

This brings me to signs. The Universe was speaking to Kelly, offering a much-needed solution that would get her started on her goals. Based on old ideas, she just wasn't getting them, until she did. This demonstrates both the Universe's unlimited patience with us and its endless methods for giving us answers.

It's easier to spot an inspired action assignment when we've learned to ask for, recognize, and/or properly interpret signs. As a meme I once came across said, "There are some questions that can't be answered by Google." Our human knowledge is limited. We can't possibly see the myriad of possibilities and puzzle pieces that can come together to form a miraculous manifestation. But the Universe does indeed know. Accessing this wisdom is imperative to manifesting both joyously and efficiently.

Asking for Signs

1. **Ask.** Use prayers to ask for signs, to be shown the next step, places to look, people to contact.

    Some examples:

    Show me, omnipotent Universe, what I need to do next to create the life I desire. (Feel free to replace "the life I desire" with something much more specific like, "the most fulfilling career" or "the financial freedom I'm seeking.")

    Beloved Oneness, open my eyes so I can see all the signs around me leading me to my greatest good.

    > Nothing gets in the way of love. Generosity of spirit empowers us to perform miracles and wonders.
    >
    > **—Anthon St. Maarten**

    Sweet Spirit, I open to your signs pointing me in the direction of _____ (what you're manifesting). Give me the courage and motivation to act on the signs without haste.

    Light the path, oh Father Mother God, to me being one with _____ (wealth, true love, my perfect career, my soul's purpose).

    Eternal Light, show me a sign and make it so clear, I can only understand it.

Affirmative Prayers (see also chapter 9).

With these, you are stating in the present tense that signs are guiding you and the answers are here.

An example:

> There is one Universe, and I am one with it. This Universe is all knowing. It already knows the perfect out-picturing of this manifestation. I see signs pointing me in the right direction and giving me the next step. Every answer I need to every question, I already have within me. These answers become conscious now. I am grateful for this knowing. It is done and so it is.

2. **Oracles.** From the ancient tarot and all its incarnations to the coins of the *I Ching* to tea leaves to palm reading to numerology and astrology, every civilization and every culture throughout time has used some form of divination to interpret meaning in the world and get guidance.

   Because everything reflects what is within you, your energy draws out results based on where you are right now. The future is always changing. I have found using oracles to be most powerful when asking for guidance on present or near-future circumstances.

   If oracles are new to you, I would pick a method or modality that is simple, positive, and encouraging. Approach asking by letting go of attachments to what you want to hear. (How? Intend. "My intention is to release all attachments to the outcome. I am open to true guidance to help move me forward on my manifestation now.") If you're not clear what the oracle means for you, ask for clarity. Whatever sign you get, take a deep breath and journal about it. Some additional guidance may unfold through writing.

3. **Life itself as an oracle.** There are many benefits to getting extra observant to life unfolding all around us. In the past, this would have been a normal survival skill. Awareness kept people safe. Now, we are so often in our heads or on our phones, we are missing out on how the Universe is trying to communicate with us every single day. And if you're praying for a sign, this is where those signs will be shown. Step 1 is pay attention.

It can look like the words on a billboard, bumper sticker, or business sign. A spam email showing up in your in-box. A red fox crossing in front of your car. A book falling off the shelf. Weather patterns. Be open and you will find the Universe is incredibly creative in getting information to you.

4. **Ask.** Yes, again! Ask to be shown the meaning. Ask for clarity. Ask for rock-solid knowing.

Recognizing Signs

Repetition

It's a good thing the Universe is infinitely patient with us. There are times I observe my own clumsy, confused, distracted humanness and think, *Man, the Universe has its work cut out for It.* Fortunately, signs are often repeated until we get them.

Examples:

Three people who don't know one another mention the same book to you. (If this happens, I would say it's worth checking out.)

You're wondering if you should take a pregnancy test. You see a mama duck with her babies, a horse nursing its foal, and a "Puppies for Sale" sign all in a fifteen-minute drive. (I'd get on that.)

You're deciding between a job in San Francisco and Chicago. You see an ad for Chicago-style pizza. The front page of the *Chicago Tribune* blows onto your car window. And you live in Des Moines! A friend offers you a ticket to a local production of *Chicago*. (I hope you have snow boots.)

> Our lives are stories built of small moments. Ordinary experiences. It is too easy to forget that our days are adding up to something astonishing. We do not often stop to notice the signs and wonders. The writing on the wall.
>
> —Christie Purifoy

When anything comes up a minimum of three times, this is worth exploring. If you've received two similar signs, keep your eyes open for number three. Or ask the Universe: Is this a sign? And see if you get a confirmation.

Strengthening Intuition

List all the times you've had an intuitive hunch.

For each memory, document the situation's details and how you experienced the intuitive impulse. Was it a feeling? A vision? A phrase you heard in your ear?

Then write if you followed it or didn't, why or why not, and what happened as a result.

Don't use this assignment to be hard on yourself. If there were times you did not follow your intuition (after all, who hasn't?) and it cost you, it's imperative to forgive yourself. Examine the reasons for why you didn't follow it, like it wasn't logical, practical, or you didn't want to hurt another's feelings. If you're aware of what tripped you up before, you'll be less likely to repeat it.

Interpreting Signs

If a result comes up that you don't understand, sit with it, meditate on it, journal about it, and ask the Universe, "Please show me what this means."

Feeling State

Otherwise known as *going with your gut.* Every person is born with intuition or gut instinct. For the highly sensitives, this will be an easy one.

1. Hold the potential sign in your mind. Mentally review it.

2. For a couple of minutes, breathe in and out through the center of your chest to move from your mind to your heart.

3. Now drop into your whole body. What does this potential sign feel like? Cringey? Yummy? Like static cling? Or a wave of champagne bubbles rising up from your toes? Or not much at

all? Allow the feeling state to show you if this is a sign or not. If it's a sign, is it telling you to move forward or to forget it?

MANIFESTING MINI PROCESS

Documenting Signs

You and the Universe will develop a language between you, and signs are a part of that communication. Document the ones you receive, how you interpreted them, and how accurate you are. You'll start recognizing patterns in what you're receiving.

That's what I love most about signs. They are evidence from a loving presence that we are seen, known, and guided. Don't just use them for important decisions. Ask for input each and every day.

11

Manifesting Alchemy Practice 4

THE ART OF LISTS FOR MANIFESTATIONS

By far, one of my favorite and most popular manifestation processes. Lists work!

As a child with attention deficit disorder, I gravitated toward lists at an early age. I don't know many second graders with itemized to-do lists, but that's who I was. Placing the things I needed to do on paper not only prompted me to get them done, but I could then organize their order for maximum efficiency. It also reduced overwhelm. Instead of mentally juggling tasks, I could see them laid out before me. Suddenly, everything felt more manageable.

1. **Master Manifestation List.** Create a list of a hundred things you want to do, be, and have. Leave out the "before you die" bit. This is not a bucket list per se. Really stretch here.

   What do you want to do?

   Travel to Thailand, learn ukulele, jump out of a plane?

What do you want to be?

An audiobook narrator, best crêpe maker in California, an advocate for foster children?

What do you want to have?

A cottage by the ocean, a Vespa scooter, stained-glass windows?

2. **"This year, I desire . . ."** Make a list of things you want to accomplish over the next year. Do not wait for New Year's Eve or your birthday; start anytime.

Actor-comedian Tiffany Haddish publicly shared a story of how her colleague Kevin Hart helped her accomplish incredible career goals. At the time, things were dire. She was living out of her car, unable to afford an apartment, trying to make it in comedy. Kevin gave her $300 for a hotel room. He told her to make a list of what she wanted to do in her career. With nothing left to lose, she made the list. After that, immediately her circumstances began to change. She got a call about a very cheap apartment that was just what she was able to afford. Opportunities began opening up. And now she's an actor in major movies and featured in her own comedy specials. She accomplished everything on that list, including becoming friends with Will Smith and Jada Pinkett Smith, and much more!

On January 5, 2018, my birthday, I quickly created a list of what I wanted to accomplish that year. "Write a book" was included. I had wanted to do just that since I was eight and first fell in love with the written word. I could express on paper what I was unable to say out loud. Yet in all these years I had not done it. Recent developments in the world of self-publishing that had streamlined the process felt promising for me. But at the time I made the list, this goal seemed unlikely. I was in a new living space, traveling, and expanding my healing business. When would I find the time to write a book? And on what? I could easily write on a hundred topics, but nothing seemed to be on the top of the list. I just couldn't narrow it down. Less than two months later, I was asked by St. Martin's Essentials to write a book on energy healing. No book proposal, no agent, no outline. And this is a topic I don't just know but live. I wrote it in six weeks. My schedule suddenly cleared, giving me the space I needed to get it done. A year later, I was a legimate author, with a most well-respected and prestigious publisher. One of my favorite things to do when I travel is visit bookstores and find my book on a shelf. Signing it makes me incredibly happy! The Universe had a bigger idea for me than I had for myself. When I was speaking with a literary agent and shared my publishing story, he kept saying, "This is highly unusual. Most unlikely! I can't believe this is how you got a book deal. It never happens this way!" It's not the first time someone has said that to me when I've shared my favorite manifestation stories. What I want to say to you is this: It *can* and *does* happen. It happened for me.

3. **The Best List Manifestation Process . . . Ever!** I have taught this process to thousands of people. And it's the one I get the most frequent and exciting feedback on. If you're reticent to try the others, start with this baby. It's ideal for left-brained, linear thinkers and newbie manifestors as well.

   a. Choose something you'd like to manifest. This works well with tangible, concrete items like living spaces, cars, jobs, and yes, you can use it to attract a mate as well.

   I'll use manifesting a new house as an example.

   b. Start your list with a couple of general affirmations that acknowledge the power of the Universe and your connection to it.

   c. Title it: My _____ (new home, job, etc.)

   This claims the manifestation as already yours.

   Example: My New House or My First House

   d. Start listing all the qualities you'd like in this manifestation, from most important aspects on top and lesser important items as you go down. Begin each item with "My."

   "My first house is in the perfect location. It's less than twenty minutes from my job."

   or

   "My first house is in Montclair on a quiet, tree-lined street."

Think of every possible aspect.

With a house, you'll want to include location, cost, number of rooms, square footage, location to employment, stores, friends and family, type of neighbors, level of privacy and quiet, the quality of heating/cooling units, windows, walls, flooring, and doors.

A word on cost. When manifesting anything that requires money, use *affordable* versus a numbered amount. This is because what may be affordable as you start the process can differ when the manifestation materializes. Once, I jumped from a very cheap, unsafe apartment to one that was much larger, very beautiful, and had a wraparound porch and backyard. It was also $200 more per month. I was nervous about making the leap. Then I got an unexpected raise. The difference in my take-home pay was $300 per month, exactly what I needed for the rent and utilities increase. What was affordable when I began expanded once this gem of a home arrived.

e. Now include the words *This or something better.* This gives the Universe full permission to create an even better outcome than what you had in mind.

f. Express gratitude for the completion of this manifestation. Yes, in advance.

g. Use a closer:

"And so it is."

"It is done."

"Amen."

h. Print it and read it out loud every night before going to sleep and every morning upon waking.

Extra:

Infinity Energy Exercise

Take your hand and trace a sideways figure-eight pattern repeatedly in the air in front of you while you read the list.

This enhances left-and-right-brain connectivity, which is powerful in manifesting. You can also use this in other processes as well.

i. Update and revise the list. The list isn't complete until your manifestation is complete. As you get clearer about what you want, add those items to the list and reorder in importance. When you encounter what you don't want, add the positive opposite of that to the list. Print and use the updated version each time you make a change.

When I was looking to purchase my first house, I revised my list after each viewing. One home had old, drafty windows. I added "New, well-insulated windows" to the list. When I saw a home with a large kitchen, I added that to the list. Each experience was research to see what I liked and didn't.

Here's What the List Can Look Like

The Universe is all powerful and the source of everything.

The Universe and I are one.

**My First House
(ordered from most to least important)**

My first house and its taxes and maintenance are easily affordable.

My first house has 3 bedrooms and 1.5 bathrooms on two floors.

My first house is filled with a lot of natural sunlight.

My first house is in a quiet, safe neighborhood of kind, like-minded, and helpful people. I feel welcomed immediately.

My first house has a large, updated kitchen, with many cabinets, good-quality appliances, and great flow.

My first house has effective insulation so it's cozy in the winter and cool in the summer.

My first house is five miles or less from my job.

My first house has a large backyard with healthy shrubs and at least two tall trees that provide shade on hot days.

This or something better.

Thank you, beloved Universe, for my ideal first home.

And it is done now.

12

Manifesting Alchemy Practice 5

MINDING THE MONKEY MIND

What Are You Thinking About Most of the Time?

For most people, thinking is set to automatic. Some thoughts pass through. Some stick and stick hard. At any time, your mind could be bouncing around with no focus at all. One moment, you're reliving a childhood humiliation, like when a girl pretended to like you and then all your schoolmates laughed. Next, you're lamenting about what to make for dinner. Then you remember you forgot to pay the utility bill. And now you're reviewing what happened in the last episode of your favorite television show.

Is it any wonder we're not creating what we want?

Our thoughts are either stuck in the past, and that includes yesterday, problem-solving in the present, or managing our ever-growing lists of tasks and responsibilities to be accomplished in the future.

To use thoughts to create, it's important to:

1. **Appreciate what's in the present**

2. **Open up to and imagine what you desire in the future**

In my thirties, I spent a decade studying shamanism. I found it valuable to explore ancient spirituality that likely existed thousands of years before the birth of religions. Native people from all over the world, who were unable to communicate with one another in any known manner, often cultivated and utilized extremely similar spiritual and healing principles and practices. This was very intriguing to me. How is it that people separated by great distances "somehow" created similar beliefs? I believe that we are all connected and influenced by energy itself and and inner knowing. When I see a manifestation process being taught in similar fashions by different teachers and schools of thought, I take notice. That's because spiritual truths are spiritual truths, whether they were practiced in a ritual circa 3000 BC or on a recent law of attraction cruise.

One practice I've seen in various forms is based on tracking thoughts. You actively uncover and get conscious about what exactly you're thinking.

When I originally did this exercise, I was horrified by what I was focused on much of the time. One major revelation was how incredibly defensive my mind was. I was often mentally arguing with and defending myself against what I perceived as betrayals or insults from others. Sometimes, these offenses hadn't even occurred! For example, I had been ill and skipped a work meeting, only to imagine that not everyone present knew the real reason I wasn't there. They'd be talking about me in the lunch room, assuming I'd blown it off and that I didn't have to follow the rules. I found myself mentally guarding my honor. I conducted this defense while doing the dishes!

More often than not, these situations never even came to pass. Yet in my mind, I was Xena, warrior princess, sword in hand, rattling a battle cry to protect myself at all costs! This realization alone changed my life. When I was in these mental ramblings, I felt anxious, angry, wounded, and utterly exhausted. I got very honest with myself, tracking the origin of the pattern, healing wounds where I had felt victimized, blamed, bullied, and criticized. It required great effort but I knew my freedom was on the other side of forgiving all those I believe wronged me. And I did just that. I learned to cultivate a trust in the Universe and in life. When my mental defense trials relaxed, an interesting development occurred. I was able to stand up for myself in a way I never had, not alone in my head, but in my actual relationships. For all my former mental bluster, I was actually terrible at following through in real-life situations where I felt shamed or hurt. Now I could say everything I had always needed to express. And my inner Xena took a back seat to a newly channeled Diane Lockhart from *The Good Wife.* Confident, calm, composed, whip smart, and tremendously effective. I set healthy boundaries and insisted that I was treated with the same respect I gave others. The more I did this, the easier it became. Then a funny thing happened. Eventually, I hardly had to do this at all. The people in my life either complied or peacefully moved on. Those who left were replaced with gentler folks who respected themselves and, thus, me. Once I cultivated my inner peace, my relationships shifted as they no longer needed to reflect back to me painful past experiences. When the war in my mind ended, so did much of my conflicts with others.

I sometimes offer this exercise to clients, but not all are interested. Chloe was an unusual exception. An experienced triathlete, she was comfortable setting goals and embracing challenges. She had done years of personal growth work and didn't expect to uncover anything she wasn't already aware of. Not having what she wanted in romantic relationships had led her to me. What happened when she did this process came as a complete shock to her. She discovered how often she focused on "what she should have said." As a fellow writer, she held the power to edit, reword, explore, and even start all over again with her work. This just didn't translate in verbal conversations with others. Outside of her career, she felt slow in social situations, often struggling to express herself with the "right" words. Many interactions left her reliving them over and over again, mentally editing not only the use of words but her tone of voice and actions. Some of these "new-and-improved" conversations ended up in her stories. Her mind had compiled a catalog of every memory where she believed she'd slipped up, misrepresented herself, or bungled an opportunity for more meaningful connection. Several went back months or even years! She often relived them over and over again so habitually that she had no idea she was doing it. The memories brought up feelings of embarrassment and irritation, but her mind was insistent on "fixing" these until she got them right. Having always thought of herself as confident and an excellent communicator, it was painful to realize these thoughts went against fundamental beliefs she held in herself. But within the realization came the opportunity for real transformation. This pattern held an underlying belief that she was awkward and shy, a leftover from a short-lived childhood bullying situation. As she healed these thoughts, all her relationships changed. Now more relaxed and at ease, she not only could express herself more effectively, she was able to leave the conversations behind once over. Then she met her soon-to-be husband.

I've found the following exercise so valuable that I repeat it each year.

Minding Your Monkey Mind

1. **Set aside a minimum of a week to do this, two if you're able.**

2. **Before beginning:**

   a. **Look at your schedule and identify areas of routine.** Your commute to work, going to the same exercise class each week, your evening ritual of a glass of wine and a movie.

   b. **Purchase a package of brightly colored sticky notes.**

   c. **Purchase a very small, spiral-bound notebook you can keep in your pocket or purse.** If you're 100 percent unwilling to follow through on this, set up a note file on your phone. Label first page or top of note file: "My Thoughts."

   d. **Place the Post-it notes all over your car, home, and workspace (if allowed).** Put one on a pickle jar in the pantry. One on a framed photo in the hallway. Another in the refrigerator. Inside the drawer of your nightstand. On the light fixture in the bathroom. On a curtain rod in the living room. Get creative!

3. **Over a designated time period, whenever you see the Post-its, make a note of what you're thinking at that exact moment.** Whenever possible, as soon as possible, write down a phrase or sentence summing up that thought.

4. **You may notice that within a short time period, your attention gets used to the Post-its and they no longer are noticed.** If this happens, move them to new locations.

5. **After the time period is up, analyze your data.** If you've used the spiral notebook, you can tear the sheets out and start grouping similar thoughts together. You may have categories like, "Putting

Myself Down," "What Others Have Said," "Bad Memories," "Romantic Fantasies," or "Future Worries." This gives you an excellent assessment of what you're thinking of most of the time.

6. **Make note of the thought patterns you'd like to change.** Choose the largest or most painful one first, and apply the principles and practices in this book to transform it. Then do the rest.

13

Manifesting Alchemy Practice 6

"ACTING AS IF"—
THE POWER OF FAKING IT TILL YOU MAKE IT

Have you ever been in love? Achieved anything positively brilliant? Defeated an obstacle? If so, you may have experienced what I call the *twitterpated effect.* Coined from an expression in the movie *Bambi,* each spring the world gets twitterpated: filled with love and joy and looking for love in others. Something really fantastic has happened for you. And now everything is going your way! There's a perfect parking spot just waiting for you. A shopper opens a door the moment you arrive and gallantly holds it. You're humming and smiling! "Doesn't everything look marvelous today?" You beam. An unexpected check arrives in the mail. All the colors of sky look extra-rich. And everyone around you is responding positively to those sweet high vibes you're blasting.

There's a scene from the movie *500 Days of Summer* that beautifully illustrates this effect. Tom, played by Joseph Gordon-Levitt, wins the heart of the girl of his dreams, Summer, as played by Zooey Deschanel. After their first night together, he leaves her apartment smiling, as the Hall and Oates song "You Make My Dreams (Come True)" begins to play. The sun is shining on his face, and everyone he passes is greeting him with a smile and a hello. The fountain he walks past delightfully shoots water as if in celebration of his happiness. Grinning at his reflection in a window, each passerby joins him in a joyous dance routine. A simple walk to work made magical just by the way he was feeling.

I'm sure you've also had the opposite experience. You and your partner argued the night before. Tossing and turning all night long, you wake from a bad dream. Grumbling, you step on the toothpaste, and it shoots out onto the bathroom floor, that your dog has now walked in and is leaving a trail of it down the hallway and onto your new rug. You're already late for work, and the elevator door shuts just as you get to it. The boss blasts you for a mistake you didn't even make. In this scenario, the world around you is also responding to the vibes you're putting out. It's always doing that! But this time you're emanating a low vibration.

When I worked in a traditional office, my fellow colleagues would advise me to stay away from the copiers when I was in a foul mood. Too many times, my chaotic vibes had broken them! Not my actions, mind you. I didn't punch or kick the machines. Just my energy alone would do them in.

You don't have to wait until your next great love or stellar promotion comes along to consciously create these vibrations. You can act as if they are occurring now.

Ways to Act As If

1. **Choose your manifestation target.**

2. **Choose one of the following processes:**

   a. Letter to a Friend

   – Compose a letter to a real or imaginary friend. Instead of putting a future date, I suggest writing "The Perfect Day" in the area where the date would normally be.

   – Go into great detail about having achieved your chosen manifestation.

— For example, if it's a new love, share how you met, what they look like, how the two of you spend time together on dates, and most importantly, how this person makes you feel (cherished, adored, valued, beautiful, safe, important, loved).

— If it's money, share how much money you've created and how you're spending, saving, and investing it. How does this make you feel (relaxed, stable, excited, luxurious, generous, passionate)?

— You'll likely need to imagine in great detail to get to the feelings.

— Take a photo of the letter. Fold it up and place it somewhere safe and sacred.

— Then take those feelings on a walk.

— Bring them into the office. To the coffee shop. At dinner with a friend.

— How would you be acting if this were true? Would you grab a coffee for the receptionist? Tip generously? Offer to help a coworker with their assignment? Hug a friend having a hard time?

— If your mind and resolve wander, go to the photo and reread the letter. Juice those feelings for all they are worth.

b. Finding the Image

— For the visually oriented, find images that represent what you're creating. Searching images online will bring up many. Save them. If you'd like to do a vision board, print them out for later use. (See Manifesting Alchemy Practice 9 on page 139.)

— Read articles on the topic. Read true-life stories of people who have achieved this. Watch videos online related to the topic.

— Then imagine in great detail what this can look like for you. Arouse those feelings of having achieved this.

— Then take those feelings on a walk.

- Bring them to the family BBQ. To a board meeting. After service at church.

- How would you be acting if this were true? Would you bring extra food? Take the lead on a project? Offer to volunteer with the children?

- Savor those feelings!

Practicing good feelings just feels good. Period. If nothing else ever came of it, the practice itself would be worth doing. And time and time again, I've seen this little attitude adjustment yield fantastic results. While you're "performing," that twitterpating effect is inviting similar feeling tones and experiences into your life, making you very attractive to new people and opportunities. After all, would you give the promotion to the copy machine breaker? Haven't you tried avoiding people who are just like that? All day, every day, we are automatically energetically interacting with everyone we are in contact with, including the person sitting next to you on the train that you have never spoken with. Raising positive feelings sends signals out to others that you sure are nice to be around. And your energy is interacting with the energy of All That Is, inviting similar vibrations to be returned to you. Plus, you will likely take actions that return even more good to you.

Manifesting Alchemy Practice 7

DANCING YOUR DREAMS

Dancing Your Dreams

What I love most about this exercise is that it gets you out of your head and into your body. Embodying our manifestations not only helps them actualize faster, it will train your entire system to be able to receive them gently and easily.

When lottery winners are studied, the results are grim. Nearly one-third will file for bankruptcy within three to five years of winning. I once watched a documentary called *Reversal of Fortune*. A homeless man was given $100,000 if he agreed to be filmed. He was allowed to spend the money however he wished. Knowing how consciousness works, it was easy, and incredibly sad, to predict the outcome. The film producers connected him with a financial adviser and offered guidance, monitoring his progress. Yet within a short period of time, the money was gone. Radical changes can feel like a threat to the body, especially the nervous system. And yes, this includes the best changes! When a blessing unfolds, it can pull us out of our comfort zones. Normal everyday life feels safe. For this gentleman, collecting recycling for money each day made him happy. As much as the money seemed like the greatest gift, his consciousness was not prepared for such a windfall. This is also a perfect example of how changing circumstances from the outside without the inner work preceding it can lead to short-lived and frustrating results.

> The dancer's body is simply the luminous manifestation of her soul . . . This is the truly creative dancer, natural but not imitative, speaking in movement out of herself and of something greater than all selves.
>
> **—Isadora Duncan**

Besides Acting As If, the "Dancing Your Dreams" exercise prepares the body for manifestations. You're essentially practicing as if you already have achieved it, without any pressures that may come along with the reality. What pressures would those be, pray tell? If you've attracted a new love, pressure can surface from a number of areas. Meeting this person's family and/or children. How to navigate the first fight. The fear of it not working out. Traveling together. For a financial windfall, there's the pressure of how to spend it wisely. Or how to handle people asking you for money. To donate or not donate? If so, how much? Then there's learning the computer system in your new Tesla. That's quite a bit to manage. When practicing, it's all fun and all joy. Be playful and enjoy the process.

Dancing Your Dreams

1. **Choose your manifestation target.**

2. **Create a playlist of songs.** This is easier than ever before, with programs like Spotify and Pandora providing the world's largest jukeboxes right in your phone or computer.

   - What kind of songs?

     - Songs about that very goal you're working to achieve. Love will be easiest here simply because of the abundance of this in popular music. And I've seen clients create lists for abundant wealth, having a baby, exotic travel, or spiritual transcendence. Be open to exploring genres you normally wouldn't. For lists about having a happy family, try country. For wealth, hip-hop is a swanky destination. For spiritual connection, you can try everything from gospel to contemporary Christian to new age to yoga genres.

or

- Songs with a general uplifting essence. Life is good! The troubles are over! Everything is coming my way! I have persevered and am now a success! I'm on top of the world! I've included some favorites at the end of the chapter.

or

- Songs you really like that inspire happy memories and good times. Many people like to revisit music from their high school or college era, as it brings back feelings of youth, beginnings, and new possibility. I would be mindful of the lyrics here and choose those that uplift.

3. **Now dance!** Let the music move through you, and adopt the postures and rhythm of a person living that reality. Imagine you are that wealthy, loved, successful, healthy being, and allow the energy of that experience to be unleashed in your body and energy. Wrap your arms around the beloved you're calling in. Throw your imaginary pile of money up in the air and feel it raining down all over you. Proudly march like a person of prominence. Embody what you'd like to experience.

4. **When you're finished, sit comfortably and let your breath settle and deepen in its own time.** Then feel the feelings you created within your body. Breathe into the feelings and expand them until they have saturated your entire being and you feel happily enrobed in them.

Songs to Get You Started

1. "I Can See Clearly Now" by Jimmy Cliff

2. "I'm Coming Out" by Diana Ross

3. "Good Vibrations" by the Beach Boys

4. "Celebration" by Kool & the Gang

5. "The Sound of Sunshine" by Michael Franti & Spearhead

6. "One Day" and "I Will Be Light" by Matisyahu

7. "I Am Light" and "Strength, Courage, and Wisdom" by India Arie

8. "I'm in Love with My Life" by Phases

9. "Look for the Good" and "Love Is Still the Answer" by Jason Mraz

10. "Happy" by Pharrell Williams

11. "Money (That's What I Want)" by the Beatles

12. "QUEEN" by Janelle Monáe

13. "Titanium" by David Guetta ft. Sia

14. "I Won't Back Down" by Tom Petty and the Heartbreakers

15. "Beautiful Day" by U2

16. "Express Yourself" by Madonna

17. "The Prayer" by Andrea Bocelli

18. "Higher Love" by Steve Winwood

19. "We Let It Be" by Rickie Byars

20. "Flashdance . . . What a Feeling" by Irene Cara

21. "Stronger" by Kelly Clarkson

22. "Brave" by Sara Bareilles

23. "Firework" by Katy Perry

24. "Top of the World" by the Carpenters

25. "Raise Your Glass" and "Get the Party Started" by Pink

26. "I'm a Believer" by the Monkees

27. "Walking on Sunshine" by Katrina & the Waves

28. "Ride Wit Me" by Nelly & City Spud

29. "Butterfly" by Crazy Town

30. "I'll Stand by You" by the Pretenders

Check out a Spotify song list I've created just for you, my dear readers. You can find the link at www.manifestingbook.com.

Manifesting Alchemy Practice 8

CREATING A MANIFESTATION JOURNAL (AND GRATITUDE TOO!)

Creating a Manifestation Journal

You've probably heard about gratitude journals. This is where you document all the things you are grateful for, ideally on a daily basis. There are those that try to find brand-new items to document each day, pushing beyond the obvious. There are those that do short lists, just a few bullet points. I'm a writer, so bullet points aren't my style. Too brief! Too cold! I could wax philosophical about the way the sunbeams are hitting my curtains for days!

> You have to participate relentlessly in the manifestation of your own blessings.
> —**Elizabeth Gilbert**

I have found what makes gratitude journals magical is when what has been written creates warm feelings. It's one thing to think, *Yeah, I'm grateful for my good health.* It's another thing entirely to remember how easily you bounded up those steps earlier without breaking a sweat and how strong and powerful you felt shoveling snow. Or maybe you were so busy checking off your mental to-do list that that moment had passed you by. Why not revisit this? What does gratitude for good health feel like? Those are the feelings that will further encourage you to keep taking good care of your physical well-being.

So, yes, a sincere, feelings-based gratitude journal is always a good idea. More to follow on that.

And I'd like you to keep track of something else, something pivotal in being a master manifestor.

Document your manifestations. Your blessings. Your miracles. Call it whatever feels right for you.

It can be shocking how easily we forget after we've created something wondrous. Especially if you've healed a physical pain, a broken relationship, or a depleted bank account. Once the pain is past, the trouble behind you, it can be like there had never been anything wrong in the first place. Yes, by all means, revel in that success! Don't let it slip past uncelebrated. Track that story with all its gorgeous detail. Write. It. Down!

All along, we have talked about working with our conscious minds, that doubting Thomas in our heads that's pretty much convinced us all of this could just be plain nonsense. We ignore our conscious minds with their nagging doubts at our own peril. Better to subdue that monkey mind with specific real-life evidence. Especially if the manifestation in question feels very much otherworldly. Try your hand at explaining the unexplainable. Putting it down on paper can assure yourself that the mystery and majesty of the esoteric *can* indeed be real.

What successes have you experienced so far?

- State the original problem briefly.

- Document what you did to manifest a solution or different experience.

- Describe the results in great detail using sensory words. What happened? How did it feel in the moment? How did it feel afterward?

A couple of real-life examples from former students:

"I had $3.00 left in my checking account and wouldn't be paid for another ten days. I really needed gas money and started to panic. First, I used journaling to calm the panic. Then I imagined I was driving on a short road trip. The weather was gorgeous, window open, breeze whipping through my hair. I stopped for gas and easily filled up. I also prayed, knowing I was safe, and all would be well. I felt a great sense of calm and trust come over me. Then four days later, I got a check in the mail from my car insurance company. They had been overcharging me and, realizing the mistake, were refunding me $327.00! I remember holding that check in my hand and just starting to cry with relief. I felt electricity running up and down my spine, like when I hear a favorite song. It was like I was cocooned with love and care from the Universe. I was able to get gas and groceries and pay an outstanding bill. At the grocery store, I treated myself to my favorite olives.

> Be in a state of gratitude for everything that shows up in your life. Be thankful for the storms as well as the smooth sailing. What is the lesson or gift in what you are experiencing right now? Find your joy not in what's missing in your life but in how you can serve.
>
> **—Wayne Dyer**

My friend Jane said she's never heard of an insurance company admitting a mistake. I told her it was a miracle, and as I said it, I knew it was."—MJ

"My car was on its last wheels. It kept failing inspection, and my mechanic said it would be more than the car was worth to fix it. I created a list of all the qualities I wanted in a car, emphasizing affordability. My brother called out of the blue. He asked, 'Do you need a new car?' His new next-door neighbor was a repo man who was sometimes left with cars he needed homes for. I met him the next day, and he had the perfect one for me, only charging me $500 over what was owed on the loan, which was small. The only problem with it was the inside was very dirty and smelled like rotten eggs. My brother offered to have it detailed. When I picked it up, it looked (and smelled) like brand new."—CS

These examples may seem significant. But what about everyday blessings? Include those too. When you focus on all that you have, all that's working well, more good shows up automatically.

Give yourself a gift of five minutes of contemplation in awe of everything you see around you. Get out into the world and turn your attention to the many miracles unfolding moment by moment in regular experiences. This five-minute-a-day regimen of appreciation will help you to focus your life in the direction of pure awe.

Gratitude Journal

The key to making this work is in arousing juicy feelings by savoring the details. Here's an example of a gratitude list that, in my experience, won't do much.

I'm grateful for:

- The sunshine today

- My dinner out

- Laughs with Angela

> Gratitude unlocks the fullness of life. It turns what we have into enough, and more. It turns denial into acceptance, chaos to order, confusion to clarity. It can turn a meal into a feast, a house into a home, a stranger into a friend.
>
> **—Melody Beattie**

Here's an example of a gratitude list that will attract like a magnet:

> The weather report said rain, and then it ended up being a beautifully sunny day. I felt the warmth on my skin as I met Angela for dinner at our favorite Thai place. The restaurant wasn't crowded, so we were seated right away in a spot by the window. From the start, Angela had me cracking up as she shared all these hilarious stories from her trip to Florida. I even snorted! It felt so good to laugh! Then my yellow curry came, and it was the best I've ever had. It was warm, spicy, and filled with just enough heat. I had been so hungry too! I savored every single bite. Warm is actually the perfect word to use, not just for the curry, but for the entire experience.

Can you feel the difference? You don't necessarily have to make it a story as I did, but do go into hi-def detail. Describe the blessing or that which you are grateful for and then why. Why is *this* a blessing? What makes you grateful for it?

I'm a big fan of writing just about everything down. Hello, author here. But with these everyday blessings, you can make this a mental process as you go throughout the day. Integrate it into your focusing on the good.

16

Manifesting Alchemy Practice 9

VISION BOARDS

I remember my first vision board. This was pre-internet, and at the time, the only art I could seem to manage creating was collaging as I amassed a large collection of magazines. Using a broken-open cardboard box, I began affixing photos I had torn from the pages. A woman doing yoga was in the health region, a fat piggy bank was indicating much-needed savings. I promptly stuck it up on my bedroom wall and forgot about it! Not exactly the plan. But months later, I realized, I was taking yoga at the YMCA and I had a few hundred dollars in my new savings account.

I've been using vision boards ever since.

Essentially, it is a collage of images and words that represent what you'd like to manifest. I still love the old-school versions with poster board and printed images. And there are apps and programs where you can create digital

> Your vision will become clear only when you can look into your own heart. Who looks outside, dreams; who looks inside, awakes.
>
> —Carl Jung

versions easily. The benefit of the apps is you take your vision boards with you wherever you go.

Instructions:

1. **Choose one area of your life.**

2. **Collect images, either online or from magazines, that represent both:**

    a. What makes you think of and feel your connection to the Universe. This could be everything from deity illustrations to photos of candles, Buddha statues, light streaming through clouds, waterfalls, children laughing, or rainbows.

    b. What you want to create. If it's money, sure, you can print photos of piles of dollar bills. And I would encourage you to go deeper to find representations of how having more money will make you feel and what you'll do with it. Buy a new car? Remodel the kitchen? Donate to worthy organizations? Find images to match these ideals.

3. **Get a piece of poster board and arrange the Universe images in the center, with the desired manifestation all around it like the spokes of a wheel.**

4. **Place this somewhere both visible to you and not visible to anyone else.** Unless it's a dream you're manifesting with a partner or family member, like a new home. Then include them in the process.

5. **Spend some time each day looking at and allowing the images to seep into your subconscious.** Get in touch with the feeling nature of having exactly this with the Universe's support at the very center.

PART THREE

Bringing Manifesting Alchemy into Every Part of Your Life

17

Picking a Target

AREAS OF LIFE FOR MANIFESTATION

What Do You Want to Create?

There are several areas to consider when manifesting. I like to do regular check-ins with myself to assess where I am, what's working, what's not, and where I'd like to go. There is a transformative power in writing this down, even if what you document contains painful truths. Though jarring, seeing your life assessment on the page, in black and white, can give you the motivation to change it.

MANIFESTING MINI PROCESS

Where You Are and Where You Want to Go

Money

Where you are:

How much money do you earn (yearly/monthly)?

What is your current financial state?

Do you earn or have enough money to?

_____ pay for housing (rent/mortgage, taxes, utilities, upkeep/repairs)

_____ minimum or higher debt payments (if applicable)

_____ buy quality food

_____ purchase necessary clothing, household items

_____ pay for education for yourself or another

_____ pay transportation costs (car loan, public transportation fees, insurance)

_____ buy gifts

_____ save

_____ invest

_____ get health insurance coverage or pay medical expenses

_____ travel/entertainment

When you look at your bank account online or review statements, what thoughts come up, and how does it make you feel?

Which of these statements feels most true?

_____ There's never enough money.

_____ I have just enough, but I'd like more.

_____ I have more than enough and would like more.

You get a large, unexpected bill in the mail. How would you normally respond?

How do you honestly feel about people you know personally who have more money than you do?

How do you honestly feel about wealthy public figures who have much more money than you do?

What makes you feel good about money?

What makes you feel bad about money?

What are your financial desires?

How much money would you like to earn in the next year?

How would you feel if you had more than enough money for all your expenses in addition to increasing your savings and having more fun?

How much money would you like to have in savings?

What organizations or charities would you financially support?

How would you spend money on having fun?

Career

How much money do you earn (yearly/monthly)?

How did you find your current position?

What job tasks do you like most?

What job tasks do you like least?

Overall, what are the best parts of your job?

The worst parts?

How is this job in alignment and/or not in alignment with your chosen career path?

What would you like to achieve on your chosen career path?

If money, time, energy, and location weren't considerations, what kind of work would you most like to do?

What are the qualities of that dream career?

Type of hours:

Location:

Office setup:

Working alone, with another, or larger collaboration:

Debt/Financial Management

How much debt do you currently have?

How long have you been in debt?

Things You Want

Well-being:

Physical health:

Assess how you most often feel physically:

Current health challenges:

Average daily energy level? (Scale of 1–10, 10 being highest energy)

How is your sleep?

What would you like your health to look and feel like?

Physical Appearance

Things you love the most about your appearance?

Things you like least about your appearance?

What would you like to change here?

Emotional-Mental Health

Assess how you most often feel emotionally.

In what situations or relationships do you struggle emotionally?

What stresses you most?

How would you most often like to feel?

Relationships

Describe and assess your current relationships, noting what's working, what's not, and how you'd like it to be.

Work: Colleagues / creative partners / coworkers / supervisor/boss

Work: Clients/customers/students

Family:

Friends:

Life partner:

Children/grandchildren:

Animal companions:

Home

Type of housing:

Describe your living space:

How well does the size of it fit with your life?

What would you change about it, if anything?

Town:

Describe your town/city:

What do you like best?

What do you like least?

Creative Self-Expression and Hobbies

List any creative modalities you may have. (A few to consider: painting, arts and crafts, coloring, singing, writing poetry, writing a blog, weaving, home decorating, flower arranging, sewing, creating dance or exercise routines, dog training, gardening, fantasy sports, play-for-real sports, pottery, scrapbooking, drawing, beading, sculpting, and much more.)

Include ones you may have enjoyed previously, like in childhood, but haven't done in some time.

Where do you feel creatively expressed?

Where do you feel blocked?

Social Activities

Describe your typical social life:

What's working here?

What's not working?

Other Possible Categories

Evaluate what's working and what's not in all applicable areas.

Travel:

Education:

Fitness goals:

Accepting Where You Are

If these journal exercises made you feel discouraged, here are a few things to consider:

1. **You can only start where you are.** Acceptance of what is, is the very first step in changing it. Once you've stopped avoiding and gotten really clear about your current circumstances, relief awaits you on the other side.

2. **No matter how good life gets, there will always be at least one area that could use healing, improvement, or radical change.** Give up on the notion of perfection. Our souls are perfect, whole, and complete, no matter what. Our human experience? Not so much! Energy is always in a state of expansion and contraction, so our only consistency is change. That can make for messiness.

When everything feels just so right, I can guarantee another change is coming. Knowing this can be very freeing. You'll never be done creating your ideal life and your ideal life can and will change.

Let's talk about my old friend frustration. If your life circumstances don't look the way you'd like, and that's highly possible if you're reading this book, then you may know this feeling well. You may have tried to change your life in the past and not made substantial progress. It may have left you feeling like you're pushing against the current of life, only to be dragged further out to sea, defeated and confused.

How would I know? True confession time. Hi, my name is Kris, and I am a frustration-aholic.

Start with an easily frustrated temperament, add a take-charge personality, mix in a whole lot of stubbornness, while being an advanced student from the School of Hard Knocks, and here you have me. Why I also developed such high expectations for myself and life, I do not know, but it has certainly added to it!

How I healed this was by regularly practicing acceptance of what is. It's a concept shared by many spiritual disciplines. There's that popular cultural mantra of "It is what it is." When the words accompany an actual authentic feeling of acceptance, that alone can help move you into peace. On the other hand, if you say or think this while feeling resigned or angry, it won't do a thing. Feeling discouraged, halted, and sometimes enraged had not changed a single thing in my life. It simply made me more and more frustrated. I became the mythical Sisyphus, forever pushing the boulder up the mountain, only to have it roll back down to the bottom. I learned that facing the truth, exactly as it was, allowed my manifesting efforts to move forward. Once the current reality was no longer being resisted, change was now possible.

> Thought is the fountain of action, life and manifestation: make the fountain pure, and all will be pure.
> —James Allen

No matter who you are or what your life is like now, there is good to be acknowledged and savored. I know that because you have this book. Either you purchased it, borrowed it from a library or friend, were given it as a gift, or found it. You hold in your hands information. And if you have this information, you likely are able to read or view other important information. Once you make peace with what is, it's easy to realize just how much good you already have.

And if you're experiencing any resistance to what is, I recommend doing one of these processes before moving forward. You can return to them anytime "what is" feels maddening or unbearable.

MANIFESTING MINI PROCESS

Practices to Accept What Is

Affirmations

I deeply and completely love and accept myself, exactly as I am right now and as I change and grow.

I accept my life as it is right now, and it is changing for the better each and every day.

I am worthy of my own approval, and I accept myself now.

I appreciate all the good in myself and love that it grows.

I see all the good in my life and know I am blessed in every way.

My life is very good now and getting better and better every day.

I forgive myself and embrace all that I am.

MANIFESTING MINI PROCESS

Guided Meditation

1. Get into a comfortable position.

2. Close your eyes and begin to focus on your breath as you breathe normally.

3. After a minute or so, deepen your breathing in a way that is still comfortable.

4. Imagine you are breathing in and out through the center of your chest. Do this for about ten complete breath cycles.

5. Speak directly to your subconscious mind: "Subconscious mind, show me what my life is like for me now."

6. Be open to what comes. It may be an image of a teenager's messy bedroom, a stormy sea, a garden with a pile of trash in the center. You may also hear a word or phrase like *Off* or *Turned upside down.* Allow whatever information is there to come forward rather than making it happen. If you're new to working with the subconscious, this may feel challenging as your mind scrambles to "fill in the blank." If you don't get anything coming through, work with what you actively think an image of your life could look like.

7. As you hold this image or phrase, scan your body and see how it feels. Find any areas of tightness and discomfort. Breathe into those areas.

8. If you don't feel anything in your body, breathe into the image or thought. Just imagine being able to do this.

9. Say to yourself, "This is how it is just for right now. I accept this. I look for the good. And I allow my life to change for the better in every way."

10. Get in touch with a feeling of compassion, like you would feel for babies or animals. Now apply this compassion to your body and to the image.

11. Tell yourself, "I accept what is with compassion and I am moving forward with ease and grace."

MANIFESTING MINI PROCESS

Hugging Up

A variation on the guided visualization above:

1. Get into a comfortable position.

2. Close your eyes and begin to focus on your breath as you breathe normally.

3. Deepen your breathing in a way that is still comfortable.

4. Imagine you are breathing in and out through the center of your chest. Do this for about ten complete breath cycles.

5. Speak directly to your subconscious mind: "Subconscious mind, show me what my life is like for me right now."

6. Be open to what comes. It may be an image of a teenager's messy bedroom, a stormy sea, a lush garden with a pile of trash in the center. You may also hear a word or phrase like *Off* or *Turned upside down.* Allow whatever information is there to come forward rather than making it happen. If you're new to working with the subconscious, this may feel challenging as your mind scrambles to "fill in the blank." If you don't get anything coming through, work with what you actively think an image of your life could look like.

7. Wrap your arms around yourself and imagine you are hugging this image. If you heard words, see them scrolled on a piece of paper and embrace it, hearing the sound of it crinkling in your arms.

8. Feel the sensation of being both the giver and receiver of this tenderness and compassion.

9. Rock your body gently back and forth until you feel soothed and peaceful.

10. Tell yourself, "I accept what is with compassion and I am moving forward with ease and grace."

Blow It Out

1. Get into a comfortable position.

2. Close your eyes and begin to focus on your breath as you breathe normally.

3. Deepen your breathing in a way that is still comfortable.

4. Bring to mind a specific part of your life that isn't working the way you'd like presently.

5. Feel the resistance. The frustration. It may feel like a furrowed brow, a lump in the throat, tightness in the chest, a knot in the stomach, or pain in the lower back.

6. There's a number of ways you can release this. Choose what feels best for you:

   a. Breathe in and imagine blowing out the frustration onto a clean sheet of paper. Tear the paper into tiny pieces, place it in a small brown paper bag, and burn it in a safe fireproof container, preferably outside. Watch the smoke carrying the frustration away. Or go to a moving body of water and release it. (Don't worry. Paper is biodegradable.) Watch as it drifts away.

   b. Go into the woods. Pick up a rock and blow your frustration into it. Then throw it as far as you can. Say, "I am letting this go and moving forward."

18

Levels of Manifestation

You're relaxing at home when you're struck with a sudden craving for your favorite meal. You think of the restaurant that serves it. You imagine what the dish looked like that last time you ordered it. You remember the savory scents and the sensation of steam rising off the searing-hot plate, and your mouth begins to water. The meal's flavors and textures feel alive in your mouth.

You know one thing for sure. You're going to get that meal.

Here are the different levels for how this manifestation process can unfold for you.

Level 1. Trudging (most effort):

You call the restaurant, place your order, pay with your credit card, and go retrieve it.

There's the thought, the physical sensation of the craving, and you take every action to make it happen.

Level 2. Some effort:

You call the restaurant, place your order, pay, and ask for your partner to pick it up.

You've put the manifestation into motion and enlisted another's help in getting it done.

Level 3. Less effort:

You mention the craving to your partner, they order, pay, and pick up.

A little enthusiasm for the future feast, and the rest is done for you.

Level 4. No effort:

Without you taking any outward action, your partner arrives home with the craved meal in hand. They just had a feeling you'd be hungry and followed through on the impulse.

Your effort was on the invisible level and manifested on the physical, seemingly on its own.

Level 5. Megawatt manifestation:

The meal materializes out of thin air, onto a plate in your kitchen, like magic.

This is the kind of manifestation some spiritual masters like sages, saints, and gurus are said to have been able to do.

When we start on a path to conscious creation, there are some who will believe that it isn't manifestation unless it's the megawatt variety, while few achieve this level of power, myself included. When you look at the lives of megawatt manifestors, there's a reason they were people who lived lives of constant spiritual study, practice, with endless devotion. It likely requires just that! Megawatters lived in quiet isolation in monasteries or ashrams, where their only job title was: Lover of God. These masters didn't have careers where they fretted over loss in their 401(k) or whether their company would survive a recession. They didn't have a spouse complaining about noisy neighbors and a much-needed kitchen overhaul. And they certainly weren't changing dirty diapers, getting help for a child's learning disabilities, or researching colleges. Celibacy has surprising advantages!

When you start creating, focus on the end result. Did you get that meal? Great! That's what's important. It happened. You wanted it and you got it. Celebrate that. It doesn't matter if it was a Level 1 or a Level 4 manifestation. Mission accomplished.

Most often, you will need to take outward action, sometimes more, sometimes less. In the beginning, it's often more action. After creating with consistency and diligence, there will be a time when you realize you're achieving more and more Level 4s. You will simply think of something, and it will show up in your experience. Know that all beginning efforts are not just fueling your immediate target but creating a cumulative effect for future endeavors. Your confidence in yourself and the Universe grows. Your beliefs in possibilities expand. Along the way, you've been clearing out old narratives about yourself and the way life works or didn't. Now every area of life starts working more easily.

A few years ago, I was cleaning my then house when a single thought came to mind. *I'd like a cat that looks like a cheetah.* It passed in and out of my head. Now, I wasn't in the market for a new cat. Not at all. As I spent time being conscious of my thoughts, in meditation and contemplation, this seemed like just another random one, not connected to anything important. I literally didn't give it a second thought. Then a week later, on a brutal, rainy night in late October, I heard a high-pitched, panicked cry coming from outside and directed toward my front door. When I investigated, a tiny, malnourished kitten popped out of my drenched hedges and ran toward the door and into my arms. She was mere skin and bones, and I knew there was no way she would make it through this bitter night. I brought her onto my porch and got a towel to dry her off. It was only then that I noticed she had spots on her side, like a mini cheetah. In addition, she came bearing a deformed front leg. My logical mind went into overdrive. *I don't want another cat.* (But I kind of did.) *She's got special needs and is going to require so much veterinary care.* (She doesn't and didn't.) *My partner won't want her.* (He didn't. Initially. But then she outlasted him!) *My other cat won't accept her.* (She did. Wholeheartedly.) *This isn't going to work!* (Fast-forward to the happy ending: it did.) As much as I tried to talk myself out of the blessing, it was clear. She was *meant* to be with me. Her name: the Baby Cheetah. It had all been given to me in that single thought. Nicknames: the Cheet-Machine, Cheetah Rivera, and Queen Bossy Pants. Her leg didn't need to be amputated. It's used for catching sparkly pom-poms and knocking around fake mice. She moves with speed like her namesake and glows with good health. Her stubborn confidence is a constant reminder to me: we are all good enough exactly as we are. She doesn't think there's anything wrong with her, and she's absolutely right. Every day, she makes me laugh. Seven years later, she is one of the loves of my life.

So did a single thought bring a spotted kitten to my door? Was she a Level 4 manifestation? Or was the thought a Universal download, a message, a hearkening of her arrival, a divine adoption request from on high? I don't think it's an either-or pondering. The thought was clearly in my first-person voice—*I'd like a cat*—and yet, when she popped up, it felt otherworldly. It was like the thought of her came from a deeper place than where my normal thinking resides. She wasn't a conscious request. It wasn't that I was playing with my other cat and thought, *Oh, this black one, her fur is so boring. I'd prefer one in a nice jungle print.* Yet the Baby Cheetah clearly has filled a need I didn't know I had. The thought met a need, in this case an unconscious one, which met a dream resonating within me. A dream of more connection and unconditional love. Manifestation occurred. I didn't even contemplate that that dream would be filled by a tiny, seemingly compromised little fur baby. I do know as soon as I saw her sweet spots, that solo thought came back, reverberating chills throughout my entire body. I promise it wasn't just because I was damp from the cold rain. There was an immediate resonance, a full-bodied knowing. I've learned to listen to those. Deliberately creating develops thinking beyond the left, conscious brain. It enhances an energetic knowing, our intuition, that exists beyond logic and often defies it. I had every cause not to take her in, so many sensible, practical reasons for saying no. But my energy field said yes.

Trust what falls in your lap. Let the Universe surprise and delight you, even if it's not what you had in mind.

> I love the sea's sounds and the way it reflects the sky. The colours that shimmer across its surface are unbelievable. This, combined with the colour of the water over white sand, surprises me every time.
>
> —John Dyer

19

Money

I don't think there's any other topic that is as loaded as money. People love it, hate it, fear it, crave it, chase it, and are willing to sell their souls for it. We project so much onto it that has nothing to do with money itself.

Money is a unit of energy. It's what we use to assign value to and exchange for goods and services. That's it.

Common Misconceptions about Money

Money Is Limited

This is my favorite misconception to clear up about money. It's not limited. It's not as if there is one pie and if another receives or creates a larger slice, there's less pie left for everyone else. Wealth is created and grows. Pies multiply. There is more than enough for everyone.

If you create a hefty pie slice for yourself, it's not hurting or taking away from anyone. In fact, if you choose, your excess pie resources can be used to supply schools, support artists, fund medical research, stock universities, or build a hiking trail in Alaska.

> There are people who have money and people who are rich.
> —Coco Chanel

Every day, we are the recipients of the shared generosity of all. Those tax dollars that pave and fix roads? Pay for police and firefighters? Compensate teachers? These are examples of our pooled wealth.

It Is Better to Give Than Receive

Actually, both giving and receiving are really awesome. Taking the receiving out disrupts the creative flow. And it doesn't make any logical sense. You have one hundred dollars and give it away. You do not receive any additional money. How can you keep giving with nothing left? It doesn't work. Embrace both ends of the process and see them as feeding into one another. (For more information, see Manifesting Alchemy Principles 3 and 4).

Money Is the Root of All Evil

This may be one of the most misquoted Bible references of all time. It's actually, "The *love* of money is the root of all evil." The word *evil* may be a tad dramatic. I would say loving money over the Universe is always a mistake. Money is just an outlet for spiritual energy. Above all else, love the source of creation over the creations themselves. Learn to appreciate money without being attached to it. And love the Universe for allowing it to show up in your life.

Money Is Not Spiritual

Take a couple of thousand years of vows of poverty and we get this stubborn myth dominating the collective consciousness. Let's get this straight right now: everything is spiritual. Everything? Everything! Everything that exists or will ever exist comes from one infinite, unlimited source, and that source is a spiritual source. So money is automatically included. You can take the same amount of money and choose to fund political spammers or an orphanage in India. The money is a form of neutral, spiritual energy. If you're a good-hearted, loving person, you'll likely do good and loving acts with money. I'd love to see all spiritual people overflowing with abundant wealth because it would change the world in extraordinary ways.

Ways to Increase Your Financial Flow

Give What You Want to Receive

This is where the concept of tithing comes from. From a religious perspective, people who tithe give 10 percent of their income to their churches. From a spiritual perspective, giving a regular amount to the source of inspiration is a way of increasing financial flow.

Energy is either flowing or stagnant. Money is a unit of energy that increases when there is flow. Giving is the best way to increase flow.

What to Do If You Don't Have Much Money to Give

No matter what your financial situation is, give. Start small. Figure out what 1 percent of what you have amounts to. And find a place to give it that is meaningful for you. It doesn't have to be a religious or spiritual recipient. Is there a cause you would like to support? Give there. You could also choose a person in your life and gift it to them, even anonymously if that makes it more comfortable. No matter how small the amount, it could do good somewhere. Let go of the outcome and just give. See what happens. Did that 1 percent break you? Did you even notice

> Do what you love and the money will follow.
>
> **—Marsha Sinetar**

it was gone? How did it feel giving this? If there was any result you experienced due to the giving, what was it? (Your friend burst into a big smile and gave you a huge hug. The organization sent a lovely thank-you note.)

Once you realize that this giving did not harm you in any way and may have even helped both yourself and another, your "giving confidence" begins to grow. Go up to 2, 3, or 4 percent. Document what happens. As more money comes in, allow your giving to grow.

There are many spiritual teachings that believe tithing has to be 10 percent. I have experimented with this for years, and I don't believe the exact number makes any difference. What's important is that as you receive, you take a bit and give it back out. Those percentages will likely fluctuate. And what's key here is to give always with freedom and joy. If 10 percent feels paralyzing for you, then you should certainly *not* do it. Either reduce the fear until it's comfortable or start smaller and work your way up until your financial confidence has grown.

Other Ways to Give: Time and Talents

Time

If you're low on money, you may be high on time. Perhaps business is in the off-season or you're currently unemployed. After spending time on job searching and networking, see where you can invest your time to help someone else. Volunteer at a soup kitchen. Assist a friend in clearing the garage. Help an elderly neighbor plant their flower garden. As you share your time, remember, you're giving back to the infinite spirit in each person. As you give, so shall you receive.

And even if you believe you don't have time, I'm going to encourage you to do the "Time Budget" exercise that follows. It may show that you have more free time than you imagined. It can also show you where you spend time that you'd like to use differently.

Time Budget: Where Do You Spend Your Time?

Time is extremely valuable. The better you budget your time, the more you have for all that is most meaningful. That includes manifesting! And I haven't met anyone yet who said, "Oh, I have plenty of time for this." It's always the opposite. It's always, "When will I have time to do this?" There is an addiction to busyness happening, and it's not just robbing our joy but our precious resource of time. Tracking where and how you spend your time can be illuminating.

MANIFESTING MINI PROCESS

Keep a Time Journal

Spend a week writing down exactly how you spend each waking hour of time.

Put a check mark next to all activities that are necessary. Like your work hours, for example. For self-employed people, this will be a bit more complicated. There are times you may be doing that which you believe is necessary, but actually isn't.

Note how much time is spent:

Surfing the internet / perusing social media

Watching TV/movies

Socializing that's more obligatory than enriching

Anything else that's not necessary

Make a commitment to use some of your free time for activities and practices that will move your life forward.

Don't give up your internet/movie time, but limits are always a good idea. We've all had the experience of getting online, and suddenly, several hours have slipped by. Set a timer so you're conscious of how much time you're spending.

Talents

Each of us possesses skills or talents that come easily. My financial friends can simply glance at a budget and see what's working and not. For me, I just see a page with numbers. Yet I can easily help others edit their writing and have done so many times. It's actually a joy to edit another's words for a change! It flows with almost no effort. It's actually fun for me. Giving doesn't have to be drudgery. In fact, I believe the feelings you have when sharing your talents are just as important as the act itself. Find what you're good at, and be willing to share these gifts you've been blessed with. Share with enthusiasm and joy!

See the next chapter for Manifesting Reflection Questions on Talents and Skills.

Get Excellent at Receiving

I started out telling you to give and receive in equal measure. Then proceeded to say *give, give, give.* I wasn't done yet!

Please see Manifesting Alchemy Principle 3: Deservability and Open Receiving. It's an extremely important principle to embody. There are tips there for learning to receive well. Here are some additional ones.

Enhance your receivability by claiming it.

"I am wildly open to receiving every conceivable good."

"I lovingly claim all that is already mine by Divine Providence."

"I am worthy to receive, and I receive generously."

"All that I've given returns to me multiplied abundantly. I happily receive it all now."

"It is good to receive."

Savoring Gifts

Anytime you receive, savor every single thing that is good about it. Even if it's, say, a hideous orange-and-green-striped sweater from your mother that has you questioning her sanity, find the good anyway. She was thinking about you. She didn't want you to be cold. She spent money purchasing and shipping it to you because she thought you'd truly enjoy it. Thank her enthusiastically. And put it back into flow by finding a person or organization that can use it.

See Abundance Everywhere

I pick pennies up off the ground whenever I see them. It's like they've become disposable currency! Money is not garbage. If I focus even just a bit on them, I will notice them everywhere. But a penny is a unit of energy that when combined with other units can have an impact like any other denomination. When I pick them up, I always say, "Thank you, Universe, for this abundance." I encourage you to do the same.

Abundance is not just cash. Nature overflows with abundance everywhere you look. Most plants produce far more seeds than can ever be rooted. Nature has designed it so florae simply overflow with them.

Spend time in nature observing its abundance. See the multiples of blades of grass. Notice the plethora of weeds! Rather than curse them, bless them! You pull them and they just produce more. Open up a pomegranate, and as you pull the tasty little nuggets out, see the generous abundance inside.

The tree doesn't worry its leaves will be too sparse this season. The bird doesn't panic over the source of its next meal. Nature trusts. Nature is flexible. Nature moves with change. When rivers dry up, animals migrate to new waters. Nature is a precise teacher on how the abundance of the Universe works.

MANIFESTING MINI PROCESS

Meditate with Rhythms of Nature's Abundance

Allow yourself to get comfortable and begin to follow the easy in-and-out flow of the breath.

See an empty meadow. Imagine stepping on the soft grass, feeling the warmth of the sun on your skin. A breeze gently touches your face. You hear the sounds of birds chirping as they pass overhead while you look up at the brilliant blue sky. Looking on the right side, you see green tendrils emerge from the earth and grow quickly up toward the sky as leaves and buds form, before expanding into full flowering. You look ahead, and the meadow is being filled with the lush growth of thousands of beautiful wildflowers in every color, springing up everywhere you look. Breathe the energy of this abundance into your body, reminding yourself that you are an essential part of nature, and abundance is yours now.

Allow abundance and prosperity to be your natural birthright. The Universe is your source and supply of all good, including money. It's here, and it's available for you.

> Nature is the manifestation of God. I go to nature every day for inspiration in the day's work. I follow in building principles which nature has used in its domain.
> —Frank Lloyd Wright

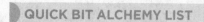

4 Ways to Turbocharge Everything You Do

1. **Write it down!**
2. **Join forces with a mastermind partner.***
3. **Visualize in a way that works.**
4. **Spend daily time in nature.**

*The concept of mastermind groups was put into print with the success principle books by Napoleon Hill, including his classic *Think and Grow Rich.* He wrote, "The coordination of knowledge and effort of two or more people, who work toward a definite purpose, in the spirit of harmony." And also, "No two minds ever come together without thereby creating a third, invisible intangible force, which may be likened to a third mind [the mastermind]."

20

Career and Achievements

We spend decades of our lives working. This includes stay-at-home parents, full-time caregivers, and other not-paid-in-money workers.

If you're retired, your life's purpose is not over. I know that because you're still in a body! This means you will likely have time to create a retirement that feels fulfilling, whether that means being in service in a new (and better) way or enjoying leisure activities that uplift rather than put you to sleep.

If you're fortunate enough to not need to work for income, then you still have time to be spent.

> Do not go where the path may lead, go instead where there is no path and leave a trail.
> —**Ralph Waldo Emerson**

This chapter is about using your time in ways that thrill you. That make you excited to be alive!

I'm continually surprised at how all that I was drawn to as a child is part of what I do now. As soon as I could crawl, I went after the magazines on the coffee table, pulling them onto the floor. My mother shared how I would look intently at the pictures as I paged through them, like they were somehow familiar to me. As a child of the '70s, I'm sure I was curious about the fashion of the time. "So this is what people are wearing now? Oh no!" When I was eleven, I began subscribing to music magazines like *Rolling Stone,* impatiently awaiting each issue so I could read it cover to cover. Later in adulthood, I had magazines coming in the mail constantly. I don't think anyone was more devastated about the loss of print media than I was (and am). Then I began the newsletter for my business. An essential part of being both a healer and small-business owner, newsletters are usually perfunctory affairs of announcements with tidbits of useful content. Not so for me. I turned the newsletter format inside out. By including music videos, poetry, film reviews, original photography, contests, downloadable handouts, and memes, along with articles on healing and class announcements, my newsletter became a passion project.

One New Year's Eve, I was torn between three social opportunities: a party, a Buddhist meditation, and a live music event. Normally very decisive, I could not understand why I didn't just pick one and commit already. I was being presented with an option for every possible mood. Then I realized something surprising. What I most wanted to do was stay home and create a newsletter for my then tiny tribe of subscribers. That's exactly what I did. This was my magazine, after all, in which I was editor, photographer, writer, and designer. I would not have wanted to be anywhere or doing anything else. As I got busy, I caught a glance at myself in the mirror, sitting in my underwear, hair in a sloppy bun, and chuckled at the thought of my so-called glamorous life. I rang in the new year filled with creative enthusiasm, doing what I love. Doing what I've been drawn to since I was a baby!

I want you to spend your time doing that which you love so much, you'd do it alone. On New Year's Eve. In your underwear.

I never actually set out to give my magazine obsession new life in my business. I began the process, learning the technology of the newsletter program, normally not one of my gifts, and within minutes, I was crafting my first edition. As I filled in the necessary blanks, ideas began popping up. *What if I hand-painted a worksheet on gratitude, attached a scanned copy, and everyone could print it out at home? What if every year on my birthday, I gave away ten copies of my favorite books? What if I shared my own photos instead of stock images?* Each idea felt like a spark. It unfolded organically. When colleagues ask me how I get my ideas, I say, "It's so easy. I just love creating my newsletter. The ideas simply just arrive and right on time."

Whenever I sat down to craft the next edition, I noticed that several hours passed in an instant. That still happens. Every. Single. Time.

Concentration without Effort

If you're not clear about what you're truly passionate about, here's a major clue:

You experience concentration without effort.

You and your passion lock into a zone of timelessness, and the concentration simply unfolds. It's not laborious or painful. No forcing. No looking at the clock. Hours pass effortlessly.

This is normally where a student will chime in with, "Okay, so I love to knit. I could do it for days. But there's no way I can make a living at that! Is that what you're asking us to do? To try to support myself with *knitting*?"

I decided to give money its own chapter for a reason. For many of us, our careers will be our main sources of financial abundance. But not always. Money can be manifested in the most extraordinary of ways. The kind of ways that seem like a movie plot rather than real life. Major inheritances, lottery and other contest wins, a significant offer for a creative project. Be open. Manifest the money, and your time is your own to do with as you please. Don't make your passions about money. Money enables you to live. Passions give you a life.

And by the way, yes, you can make a living at knitting. Or baking cupcakes. Or writing movie scripts. As many passions exist in the world, so too are the ways to monetize them. I once met a woman who was passionate about creating the perfect eyebrows. Yes, eyebrows! She created a successful six-figure business, visiting salons within a forty-mile radius of her home, shaping the eyebrows of women of all ages. The salons made the appointments and collected the money. She showed up on her specific day, worked her artistry, and got paid. Once, she showed me illustrations from her high school art classes. Oh, so many eyebrows! The teachers could not understand it. She didn't understand it. But it became her dream career. Later, she added the training of other "eyebrow artists" to her business model. Surely, if eyebrows can make a person happy and bring home the bacon, then anything can!

Let's call our doubting knitter Maria. She simply puts her love and effort into her knitting projects. Her friends don't get it. Isn't she bored? Don't her fingers hurt? Ignoring them, she continues with her projects. Then, somehow, Maria gets an idea for a new stitch. It works! She starts classes teaching this to others. To promote the classes, Maria creates funny teaser YouTube videos on topics like choosing eye-catching yarn color combinations or how size matters with needles. These YouTube videos land her on the *Today* show, where she is presented as a modern knitting expert. What follows are books, her own tool line, and a regular feature in *Martha Stewart Living*.

You may find this unlikely. But if you research biographies on successful people, many of their stories unfold like that. A person follows their passion, undeterred by the opinions (and even mockery) of others, and this passion morphs into a grander, more prosperous life. The best part is if you're spending more time doing what you love, you're not waiting for a specific outcome. You're loving the creative process all along, so as it begins to grow, you grow along with it.

And everyone has a passion. And for every passion, there are others who share in it. I once saw a bumper sticker that said, I BRAKE FOR JEW-ISH CEMETERIES. I thought, *There are enough people into this specific activity that an organization was created to support it, and they make bumper stickers to promote it.* It was a revelation.

Do you know why passion flourishes? It's because passion itself is contagious. People crave it. Are drawn to it. And need it! You become the vessel for passion, you and the object of your ardor become very attractive indeed. Passion also spreads. Give more of yourself to it, and it will sprout in every area of your life.

Steps for Manifesting Your Ideal Career, Soul's Purpose, or Leisure Time

Manifesting Reflection Questions on Talents and Skills

1. What did you love to do as a child? Include everything you can think of.

2. What social or political causes make you want to get involved?

3. If you were a superhero with incredible powers, how would you change the world? (You don't have to wait to be a superhero to get passionate about helping the world. Now that you know where you'd like to help, you can start on that now.)

4. When was the last time you contemplated trying anything new? What was it? How did you feel?

5. Think of something you've always wanted to try and make plans to experience it.

> Passion is energy. Feel the power that comes from focusing on what excites you.
>
> —Oprah Winfrey

6. What is the name of a person who you feel leads a passionate life? It could be a person you know or anyone famous or renown. Describe their qualities.

   Bonus: If you know this person, interview them about their passion. You won't be bothering them, believe me. People love to "talk shop" about their passions. Speaking about what you feel passionate about brings up juicy feelings, so it's highly enjoyable.

MANIFESTING MINI PROCESS

Passionate Purpose Visualization

You don't need to know your passionate purpose to do this exercise. You're going to allow the language of the subconscious mind to connect you with the energy of it. It won't be long until what's unconscious becomes conscious.

1. Imagine you're walking in a place that feels peaceful to you. This could be a natural setting like a beach, meadow, or cottage at the bottom of a mountain.

2. Spend a few minutes breathing deeply and consciously.

3. Imagine that as you walk, you see something up ahead. As you get closer, you notice it's a beautiful box. On the lid, it says, "My Passions."

4. Place your hands on the box and feel the powerful, swirling energy within it.

5. Get in touch with the excitement at having found this precious gift.

6. Open the lid, and allow the energy in the box to fill your heart center and spread through the rest of your body, bringing curiosity, enthusiasm, and excitement.

7. If you see any symbols or pictures, make a note of them. You may also hear sounds or feel sensations in your body. Catch them all.

8. Know that this energy has ignited passion within you.

9. After you open your eyes, ground your energy by gently tapping your feet up and down on the floor.

The coolest thing about doing this work is that passions often unfold within you that you didn't know were there. Don't get discouraged if you're not clear on this. Work on creating what you most need now, and be open to what gets ignited within you. Writing has always been a true love of mine. When I kept getting impulses, and offers, to speak publicly, I resisted it completely. "*This* wasn't in my plan. *This* isn't what I want to do!" Yet the offers, and intuitive nudges, continued. I neutralized my fears and started saying yes. Now, being a speaker fulfills a creative need in me I hadn't known I had. I absolutely love every aspect of it, from crafting a speech to taking the stage. If I hadn't allowed this passion to unfold through me and my life, I would have missed out on so many incredible experiences I've had and the opportunities it has drawn to me.

> The purpose of life is a life of purpose.
> —Robert Byrne

21

Health and Beauty

Health

Whether you're essentially healthy or struggling with a short- or long-term condition, using these manifestation principles and practices can be enormously helpful to your physical well-being.

What I've found is that I normally tolerate unease in my body for far too long, until that discomfort grows, finally getting my attention. I know I'm not alone in this. It's a side effect of busy lives. But it's important to note that it's usually simpler to heal when a condition begins rather than after it has intensified. After all, it's easier to focus when you're not in debilitating pain. A good rule of thumb is to act quickly in turning a health condition around. At the same time, don't let a long-term condition convince you it can't be healed. I have seen truly miraculous experiences unfold before my eyes. An inoperable brain tumor disappears. Cancer cells in the blood vanish. A multiple sclerosis diagnosis goes asymptomatic. A cranky gallbladder that needs to be removed stops hurting and remains intact. Vision dramatically improves. In some of these cases, the manifestor used medical treatment along with practices like the ones contained in this book. In some others, there was

> Everybody needs beauty as well as bread, places to play in and pray in, where nature may heal and give strength to body and soul.
> —John Muir

no medical treatment available for the condition, so the person relied on the power of their creative minds. And in all the circumstances I've just listed, none were expected to heal. An inoperable brain tumor is just that. This person and their family decided to reach outside the conventional to try anything that could help, and that brought them to me. A few of my prayer practitioners and myself used affirmative prayer for this person. Two days later, a test confirmed, it was simply gone. Using these processes along with any medication or treatment you are doing can only be beneficial. You don't have to wait until a seemingly incurable condition presents itself to make manifesting a part of your healing. Make these practices a part of your everyday well-being, and every facet of your life benefits, including your precious body.

There are absolutely times a surgery, medication, or other medical treatment *is* the answer to a person's healing. Always seek the advice and treatment of a trusted medical professional when needing a physical healing. You can let them know you'll be doing mind-body practices along with their treatment protocol. That may take a bit of courage. Yet I've found there are more and more doctors who are developing a deeper understanding of the mind-body-spirit connection and are supportive of such practices. The entire field of complementary medicine is dedicated to this.

> In every culture and in every medical tradition before ours, healing was accomplished by moving energy.
> —Albert Szent-Gyorgyi

I recently met my friend Mary Day at a cancer center to visit with her while she underwent chemotherapy. This hospital was a revelation to me! The lobby held a basket for prayer requests and a wire tree with colorful papers attached. Each little sheet contained an inspirational quote or saying you could remove and take with you. All patients had access to support groups, Reiki, massage, art therapy, and group classes of all types. Inside the elevator doors was a powerful message: "Inhale Courage and Exhale Fear." I can assure you that money is being invested in these innovations because there is a deeper understanding happening of the mind-body-spirit connection. People are beginning to understand that this stuff works!

Every doctor and medical researcher is aware of the placebo effect. This is where a patient is given a fake medication, shot, or procedure. They are told this fake treatment can heal their condition. Some of these patients heal, even though they did not receive any medical treatment at all. They just believed that they had. It's been recognized in medical studies for decades. It's so powerful that medication studies now have to account for it, surmising that a certain percentage of healing can be caused by this effect.

When you're manifesting for health, the results can demonstrate in a few different ways.

1. The condition transforms without you making any outward changes.

2. You get intuitive "downloads" on important specific lifestyle changes to make like diet, exercise, alternative, and/or traditional medical care, stress management, or medications and/or supplements. The intuitive information may encourage spiritual changes like learning to meditate, prayer, or finding a religious or spiritual community. Or the information may encourage you to make changes in your career, relationships, or living situation. You implement those changes and the condition heals.

3. You realize there is a painful limiting belief or memory that is behind the condition. (See chapter 24, "Dealing with Doubts and Releasing Resistance.") Heal the belief, and the condition goes away.

Don't judge the results or yourself for how this manifests. We all want option #1. That's humanness for you. It would just be so darn efficient, and cheap, wouldn't it, if all the pain just disappeared? But with options #2 and #3, I have found that when this occurs, there are additional benefits.

An example: You have psoriasis on your knees and elbows. Visualizing them disappearing, you get an intuitive idea to learn about leaky gut. As you're researching, you see you have several of the other symptoms besides the skin issues, so you implement a healing regimen for this condition. You thought it would be impossible but find you

> Knowing that we can be loved exactly as we are gives us all the best opportunity for growing into the healthiest of people.
> —Fred Rogers

have the motivation to do it after all. And not only do those uncomfortable red spots go away but you feel energized, focused, and happier than you've ever been. You're sleeping better and digesting your food efficiently. You've even released excess weight. It may have required some effort on your part. But the results are outstanding.

And you don't have to wait to be struggling with a serious illness before choosing to work on your health. There's always potential for growth, for more energy and vitality than you've felt before.

Health and Beauty Visualization

Guided visualization can be very helpful on health conditions. This process can be used to improve the appearance of beauty concerns like wrinkles, age spots, and skin elasticity. It can also be used for health conditions like improving digestion and weight.

Preparation

1. Choose a health condition you'd like to heal or improve.

2. Do some visual research. Many people outside of the medical and health worlds don't know much about anatomy. If you don't know what the lining of your intestines should look like or where your liver is located, find out. Get an idea of whatever body part(s) or system you're working on (circulatory or digestive, for example).

3. What would this organ or system look or feel like in its healthiest state? What does it feel like when this organ or system is in its healthiest state? Get the answers.

Process

1. Settle into a comfortable position.

2. Focus on your breathing, and let your body relax.

3. Imagine you're holding out the palm of your hand. In it is a golden ball of light. Place this ball of light into the body and see as it goes to the area needing healing.

4. See the light making changes. Here are some possibilities:

   • Reducing inflammation

   • Cleansing organs

- Loosening tightness in sore tendons

- Smoothing out wrinkles

- Tightening sagging skin

- Dissolving blockages

- Dissolving fat

5. Tell your cells you know they have the power to bring you back into balance. Say, "Cells, I give you permission to transform this condition back into health."

6. Cultivate the feelings you believe you'd have if this condition was improved or healed. What are they? Relief, peace, excitement? Create those feelings within and expand them with each exhalation.

7. When you feel complete, open your eyes.

Other Alchemical Practices for Health

Affirmative Prayer for Health

There is one power in this infinite Universe that has created all life, including me. I am one with this force. It is all knowing and all powerful. I know this force as _____ (the Universe, God, Life, High Self, use what works for you). The Universe is within every level of my being, including my mental, emotional, and physical dimensions. Whatever has caused the appearance of this condition, I affirm it is uprooted and completely dissolved now. I radiate vibrant health. I am a demonstration of happy vitality. All systems of the body are working together in perfect harmony. I feel and look beautiful. I'm grateful for feeling good. And so it is!

Vision Boards

Find photos of not only healthy, happy, vibrant people but symbols of what good health feels like for you. That could be a very old tree, strong and sturdy. Or a flowering vine, growing up a trellis, overflowing with abundant blossoms, demonstrating vitality and progress. Include pictures that represent the Universe for you. Get into a daydream state of mind, and gaze at it a few times a day, getting in touch with the feelings of health. For more details, see chapter 16, "Manifesting Alchemy Practice 9: Vision Boards."

A true story of healing:

I had been invited to York, United Kingdom, to present at a conference for EFT practitioners. Ever since I was a punk rock teen, I had wanted to visit England. I collected Union Jack memorabilia, including a cherished T-shirt I wore until it fell apart. Finding an underground for British music magazines, I read up on the latest groups and traded with friends. I felt a true kinship with this country I had never visited. And all these years later, it was *finally* happening. I was going to England! The hotel for the conference was the prestigious Royal York. Upon arrival, I looked out of my room's window and was delighted to see an ancient castle wall surrounding the city. I had arrived! But my joy was quickly replaced with overwhelm and fear. Almost no one at this conference had ever heard of me, and I was still an inexperienced speaker. What if I bombed? I kept getting intuitive downloads to speak on spirituality, even though that was not this type of conference. What if the event organizer regretted inviting me? And I humiliated myself in front of my colleagues? Throughout the first day of the event, I was paralyzed with fear, hardly able to take in the other presentations and connect with anyone. It was all I could do to keep from hiding under the table. I left dinner early that evening, returning to my room to review my notes and rehearse the talk. I would be first up the next morning and teaching an all-day workshop the following day.

As I read my notes out loud, something suddenly felt off. I started noticing the need to clear my throat over and over again. My nose had become terribly stuffy. As I wiped my sweaty brow, my skin felt scorching to the touch. Mind you, it was January. I felt my entire body begin to get tight and clammy. I looked in the bathroom mirror, and my face was as red as a tomato. As much as I had been trying to ignore the symptoms, the realization slapped me in the face. I was getting the flu! My body was consumed with the fire of fever. My roommate and dear friend Jondi, another presenter, got back to the room. I sat on the edge of my bed, head in my hands, and began to cry while I shared what was happening. Here I came all this way, to a place I had dreamed of for decades, for a chance to speak and teach internationally for the first time ever. And now it would all be ruined. They would have to find a last-minute replacement and I'd feel humiliated. My workshop would be canceled. Goodbye to the money I would have made which I very much needed to fund this trip. And I'd be sick and alone in a foreign country.

But, dear readers, I don't give up so easily, not even when all looks impossibly doomed. I have a whole lot of mojo-making manifesting tools in my kit, and this was the time to use them. I texted an SOS to my spiritual community back in New Jersey. They immediately began using affirmative prayer on my behalf. Jondi and I used energy healing practices together. Then I visualized myself on that stage, speaking loudly and proudly. I prayed to release the fear and to be restored to perfect health.

At this point, I knew I had done all I could do. I swallowed a week's worth of supplements and guzzled about a half gallon of water, then went to bed. I gave it all over to the Universe and surrendered. I had taken whatever action I could. The rest was up to It.

That night, the fire in my body raged. My whole being felt like a boat being tossed about in a stormy sea. The fever dreams felt like fun house hallucinations. A battle for truth versus the lies I had believed about myself was being waged in my subconscious mind. I had never experienced anything like this or since. It must be what a caterpillar feels like during metamorphosis.

In the morning, the second I opened my eyes, I knew. I was healed. My pajamas and bedding were soaked in sweat. Yet I was filled with positive energy. I wasn't even the least bit tired. My roomy vacated early to give me time to prepare. I looked in the mirror, and all I could manage to think was, *Thank you, thank you, thank you, thank you.*

> There's nothing more important than our good health—that's our principal capital asset.
>
> **—Arlen Specter**

That morning, I took the stage, and *I rocked that mic!* Without self-consciousness or apology, I delivered exactly what I wanted to say, exactly the way I wanted to say it. One thing was for certain, they had never seen a speaker quite like me! I was on fire! Not the fire of a fever but the fire of my soul's purpose. My workshop sold out. The following day, I stood for the entire day, teaching, tapping, praying, preaching, and sharing inspiring insights on healing, manifestation, and the creation process. In the window behind me, the grand York Minster could be seen as the unexpected sun illuminated the room. I fell in love with each person there. Everything was right in the world. There was no explaining it. I came to speak on miracles. And it took one to enable me to do it!

That event catapulted my career forward. Gaining much-needed confidence, I came home gushing with gratitude for the grace. There was also an unexpected side effect. I began to blow my own horn. Previously, this would have felt impossible. I didn't like to promote myself, but as one who was newly self-employed, it was now essential. Besides, what good is transformative work if no one knows about it? I was able to speak about my work with passion, sincerity, and humility. After all, I got it. There was what I could do and what the Universe could do through me.

The following year, I was invited back to speak. I got to stand on that very stage with many of the same people present. And I told them this story, tears of appreciation rolling down my face. Everything had changed for me in that year, and it had begun right there. Starting with a seeming catastrophe.

It's a memory I return to time and again when I feel lost or stuck. That night, everything aligned to bring me what I needed, so I could do what needed to be done.

Now, does this happen every time I feel like I am getting sick? I wish! Thankfully, I hardly ever get colds or flus. And when I do, it's because I have not listened to my body and responded with self-compassion. But if I could have ever chosen a time for a miraculous physical healing, that certainly would have been it.

The practices I did, and were done on my behalf, coupled with the call of my soul's purpose, aligned to make a mega-manifestation. The flu alchemized into health, well-being, and purpose.

QUICK BIT ALCHEMY LIST

3 Physical Activities That Will Open You Up to Receive

1. **Asana**
   Done at the end of yoga, this is also beneficial on its own. Lie down, shoulders back, chest open, palms up, and relax the entire body while focusing on the breath.

2. **Cardio**
   Increasing the heart rate actually allows you to receive more love. Fast walk, run, skip rope, and get that heart pumping!

3. **Serenity hold**
   Place one hand on top of the other in the center of the chest. Close your eyes and breathe deeply.

22

Romantic Relationships

For years, I taught a course on manifesting romantic partnerships. It was called Letting Love In. The title was important because most people desiring love think they just have to get out there and find it. They sign up for every possible dating site and app, hoping to finally meet that right person they click with. I wanted to make it clear from the title: love is an inside job. Being available and dating can be an important part of the process. Openness allows new possibilities. And dating can help you get clear on what you really want. In my early twenties, I really wanted to date a musician. That is until I dated a musician! Very quickly, I realized that what I thought I wanted wasn't what I actually wanted. My desires have been upgraded to better match my values and lifestyle since then. And as I grow and change, those desires continue to expand to match more and more of who I am now.

> Your task is not to seek for love, but merely to seek and find all the barriers within yourself that you have built against it.
> —Rumi

Much more than a numbers game, what I found with myself and others was that the blocks to love are actually within. Of course they are! Everything is an "in-out" experience. And there's nothing like a romantic relationship to make you feel your most vulnerable. After all, sharing a life means your person will be there when you wake up in the morning, get bad news, make mistakes, and lose your cool. They will eventually be seeing all of you, unlike the masks we wear during courtship.

And love, all love, can lead to loss. "Ah, it is better to have loved and lost than never to have loved before." Very true. Except try saying that to someone who just got dumped! The fodder for a million broken-heart love songs can't be wrong. This area of great vulnerability leaves you open to serious hurt. Those fears of being hurt are like land mines on the love journey. I watch people tiptoe around, controlling, examining, defenses up, watching for any potential wrong move. See if any of these are familiar.

Hidden Ways We Duck from Love

1. **Expecting perfection.** The new love must be the perfect everything: job, finances, height, weight, age. "She needs to have the minimum of a master's degree, make six figures, run marathons, be a gourmet cook, and own a sailboat." Whenever I would call students on this, I got the same response. "I have standards. You said I could manifest what I want." One student who was an artist came to class with a drawing of her future Ms. Right's teeth. Yes, teeth! She was sure she needed her future love to have perfect teeth just like these and felt the illustration would convince me of their necessity. All I saw was someone with inner barriers to love. I told her if Lady Golden Chompers showed up with a crack addiction, she'd likely revise her priorities.

2. **Focusing on externals.** See above. Sharing a harmonious life, including housing, finances, and family, with another person requires certain qualities. That's the practical side of love. Then there's the spiritual side of the relationship itself. Feeling seen, known, and valued seem to escape the list, but those are extremely important.

3. **Fixation on a specific person.** Admittedly, this is an easy hole to fall into. There are times you meet people to whom there is an undeniable attraction. There are many theories on who or what these folks are. I've heard them all. From past-life soul mates to living triggers of unresolved wounds to tasty temptations to

steer you from your true path to many others. They are the most valuable treasure! They are the biggest downfall! The truth is, they can be any of these. I've seen every conceivable outcome. But I do know this. No matter the circumstance, these people all have a true gift to offer: the feelings they arouse in you. You may think it's all about them. Of course you would. They have brought these feelings to the surface. But those blissful, exuberant, thrilling, passionate feelings are yours alone. And you can use them to attract the relationship of your desires. You just have to let go of it having that face. No matter how adorable. Let the face, body, name, the fact they live in the same neighborhood, so convenient! and you both went to the same college, it's destiny, right? go. Let the container go!

Free Will

A note here on manipulation and free will. In all cases, trying to manifest anything that involves the specific behavior of others is not only unethical, it's karmically unadvisable. You can hold the tantalizing contract you'd like to get in your mind without simultaneously wishing your competitor does not win it. You can focus on the qualities of love you'd like without making it "that person." Trying to make anyone the answer to your prayers is dangerous. They may be the answer to someone else's prayers. Or they may have qualities more akin to a nightmare than a dream. You just can't see it now. Focus on the qualities and feelings, but let the idea of the specific vessel go. Manipulation is bad mojo. Don't undermine the good you're creating by inviting a boomerang bang from the Universe. If this is difficult advice to follow, use the processes found in chapter 24, "Dealing with Doubts and Releasing Resistance."

When manifesting, there are times our inner control freak takes over and wants to force the Universe. I've seen this phenomenon no stronger than when creating romantic relationships. And it will never, ever get you what you most desire. When this happens, hear your inner control freak out. Let it express its demands. Then send love to this part of yourself and turn these demands over to the Universe. Surrender and offer them up. If you have to repeat this process a hundred times, then do it a hundred times. The Universe will know just how to manage this aspect of yourself so that it doesn't block love.

General Love-Attracting Principles

1. **Embrace all love.** It may not be the source you expected. It may not look the way you want. But love is all around you. When we can embrace the love we are offered in our everyday experiences, our love quotient grows. The more we let in, the more there is. The more there is, the more satiated we are. Then your person can come into a love oasis rather than a desperate desert.

   When my father passed away a few years ago, I was simultaneously going through major transitions in every area of my life. This created a perfect storm of emotional overwhelm. I went into survival mode, going day by day, moment by moment. Not always the best at asking for help, now there was no choice. I needed support. The oddest thing happened. A lot of the people I thought would be there for me weren't. And people I had never expected to offer support did. And for once, I released all criteria and expectation. I let the people who could support me do so. It was so freeing! And not only that, I didn't get bitter about the people who couldn't step forward. My needs were being met. That was all that mattered. If I had fallen into self-pity and blame, thinking, *But I was there for her and she was never there for me,* an already challenging time period would have become more so.

2. **Celebrate love.** When you spend time with couples who have the type of relationship you'd like, celebrate them. This can include famous couples as well. It doesn't mean you have to throw them a party or make your appreciation overt. Pay attention. Notice what it is about their love that is appealing. Is it the way they finish each other's sentences? Or how they speak with kindness and tenderness to one another? Is it that they always have each other's backs? Hold on to that valuable information.

3. **What you don't want.** On the flip side, notice romantic relationships that make you cringe. This will be easy enough to find. If you somehow only know happy couples, check out a reality show or two. What makes you uncomfortable? Do they seem distant and vacant with one another? Is it the barely contained contempt? Is one taking advantage of the other? Make note of this valuable

information. You'll be able to find the positive opposites of their behaviors and add them to your growing clarity on love.

4. **Forget type.** A friend of mine shared something surprising with me. He'd sworn he'd never date a Latina woman because he found them "too traditional." He told me this while sitting next to his very untraditional, independent, brilliant, and gorgeous Latina wife. We both shared a good laugh over that! In my years of teaching the course, almost every one of my students attracted a love relationship that violated some made-up rule they had carried. "I would never date anyone in a blue-collar job." "They have to be in a three-year age range as I am, plus or minus." Love can and often does come in unexpected packages. It happened so frequently, I began to wonder, where did these "rules" come from in the first place? I believe it can be the nature of resistance. It doesn't mean you don't have standards. In fact, you may need to expand those standards. It just means don't get hung up on ultimately what's not important. Your next or forever love may indeed be a short, rounded girl with red hair and glasses. Or she may be a tall, thin, willowy blonde. If it's love and the attraction is both powerful and mutual, does it matter? When you find it, you will know it does not.

Levels of Love Connection—Delve Below the Physical

1. **Physical.** This is normally where love manifestors focus exclusively. Not only does this include physical attributes like height, weight, and eye color but career, education, finances, location, age, lifestyle choices, and family of origin. I advise you to keep aspects of this general. When it comes to physical appearance, here is something to focus on or ask for that never disappoints:

   My new love is wildly attracted to me, and I am wildly attracted to them.

   Because I can assure you, this is all that matters. If magnetic, passionate attraction is important to you—and it is for most— then affirm that this is what you will feel for one another. I have dated extremely attractive men that I was not attracted to, no matter how often I told myself I should be. Let go of the package and embrace how you'd like to feel and that the feeling is completely mutual. Just thinking of them and your heart beats faster is a sweet place to focus.

With finances, I'd stay away from exact dollar figures and affirm instead:

My new love is financially responsible and secure.

Here are a few clarity questions for the physical level:

_____Describe your lifestyle.

_____How often or how little you socialize and if you'd like that to change.

_____Your eating and drinking habits.

_____Level of physical fitness.

_____Preferred types of entertainment.

_____Sleeping habits.

Place checks next to those partner lifestyle choices you'd like to match yours.

If you'd actually prefer them to have a different lifestyle, describe what that is.

2. **Emotional.** If you've suffered any romantic disappointments in the past, it was likely in this level. Everything from minor dishonesties to serious betrayals could have made you feel unsafe, disrespected, or not valued. Turn these negatives into the positive attributes you are seeking. Think about what you need emotionally in a partner.

> To love and be loved is to feel the sun from both sides.
> —**David Viscott**

What qualities make you feel at home in another's presence?

You've had a bad day. How would you like your ideal partner to support you?

As a couple, you experience a challenge. How would your ideal partner respond?

3. **Mental.** Here you'll look at shared values, problem-solving skills, memory, matters of integrity, and communication. Evaluate how important a person's intelligence is for you. Would you like a partner who's smarter than you are?

   List your core values and place a check next to any that are essential in romantic partnership.

4. **Energetic.** Energetic connection means you feel a sense of expansion in your person's presence, rather than contraction. Remember the last time you felt absolute ease and connection with another person. What did that feel like? How did you know that connection was present?

5. **Spiritual.** Consider how important it is, or not, that your person upholds similar religious and/or spiritual beliefs and choices as you. Also important is to define spiritual connection here for yourself. Perhaps you want to feel like you've known this person before. Or that the connection is otherworldly. Couples with a deep spiritual connection often feel a sense of having known each other before. What's most important for you in a spiritual connection?

Use the clarity here to create a picture of the type of person and connection you'd like to experience. Use one of the practices included in this book to bring it into form.

My 21 Favorite Manifestation Love Songs

1. "Finally" by CeCe Peniston
2. "Ring of Fire" by Johnny Cash (cover by Social Distortion)
3. "Because the Night" by Patti Smith
4. "Everything" by Alanis Morissette
5. "Chasing Cars" by Snow Patrol
6. "Soul Meets Body" by Death Cab for Cutie
7. "What Is Life" by George Harrison
8. "Nobody but You" by Blake Shelton ft. Gwen Stefani
9. "Walk Forever by My Side" by The Alarm
10. "Made Me So Happy" by Jim Boggia
11. "All of Me" by John Legend
12. "The Book of Love" by the Magnetic Fields
13. "Home" by Edward Sharpe and the Magnetic Zeros
14. "All I Want Is You" by U2
15. "Such Great Heights" by the Postal Service
16. "Question" by Old 97's
17. "In Your Eyes" by Peter Gabriel
18. "Whenever You're on My Mind" by Marshall Crenshaw
19. "Like a Prayer" by Madonna
20. "Everlong" by Foo Fighters
21. "Forever" by Ben Harper

PART FOUR

Bringing Manifesting Alchemy into the World

23

The Power of Emotion

But what about emotions?

After all, every single desire, to do, have, or be, is because of how you believe it will make you feel. Always. You think you want "it," the great job, lover, or trip. But what you really want is how having these will make you feel. Accomplished. Purposeful. Loved. Valued. Excited. Intrigued. Glamorous. Go for the feeling state, always, and your manifestation may look as you expected or be a complete surprise. Either way, you will feel how you've been wanting to feel.

One of the gifts of my private practice is I get to deeply know people from every conceivable culture, background, and status. When I work with individuals with great beauty, success, picture-perfect families, and no financial concerns, I find they still have pain. They can be as anxious, insecure, and unhappy as people with much less. What good are the goods if they don't *feel* good?

> Fear does not prevent death. It prevents life.
> —**Naguib Mahfouz**

Everyone from advertisers to politicians knows that the majority of people make decisions based on feelings rather than logic. If you asked someone why they voted for the candidate of their choice in the last presidential election, they will likely say things such as, "I just like them. They speak to me. I trust what they say." Most choose based on emotion. It's why ads try to motivate you with either fear or love or inspiration. We're either running away from something scary or toward something good. It's far easier to manipulate people with fear.

If you want to manifest like a champion, understanding and working with emotions will be a key piece of the process. When I meet people who've become fed up with the law of attraction, it's this essential knowledge that was missing from their education.

But what about negativity?

There is a huge misnomer in popular culture about negativity. You want to manifest but believe you must deny all negative thoughts and feelings to do so. If you don't, these "oogie boogies" will attract bad experiences. This has created great fear and repression in spiritual communities. And I'm here to say, this is not so. I know. I tried it that way for years, and it did not work. The more I denied the uncomfortable feelings, the worse I felt, and the worse I felt, the less I manifested. There is a better, more holistic, more grounded way to honor your emotional lives and still create what you want. And let me be clear: negative thoughts and emotions that are repressed are *not* gone. You may not be thinking or feeling them at the moment, but they still are ever present in your energy field.

First, if you're having a human experience, you will have negative thoughts and feelings. Say them out loud, don't say them, pretend they're not there, it doesn't matter. The energy behind them exists whether you give words to them or not. Your energy speaks far louder than anything you say or do. And it can only be truthful. Trying to not have negative thoughts and feelings is crazy-making. Then we develop negative thoughts and feelings about our negative thoughts and feelings! Accept and process those thoughts and feelings, and your positivity quotient will grow exponentially.

If you have a negative feeling about a family member, it came from somewhere. That energy is within you. Maybe they remind you of a parent you had a challenging relationship with. Or their behavior is hitting up against a firmly held belief. "Oh, Stephanie only thinks about herself! And no one ever listens to me." If you process what's behind that negative feeling, your reaction to this family member can change, often dramatically. So instead of pretending you feel fine around this person, you will actually *be* legitimately fine. Imagine doing that with every trigger you encounter. This, folks, is true freedom. You'll realize you don't have to go live in a cave to avoid being activated.

Second, there is a very fine line between taking responsibility for your life and blaming yourself for its experiences. I do believe we create our own realities and we are responsible for our lives. I also know that the creation process is influenced by ancestry, culture, and community, among other things. We can transform those influences that get in the way of our joy. Thank goodness for that. But if we're so busy beating up on ourselves for everything not working in our lives, we have less energy to do that.

Thoughts are much easier to manage. Thoughts are clean. You hear them. You can write them down. Then you can turn them around and come up with a positive affirmation to counteract them. When I think of thoughts, I see a man in a professional suit. Simple. Orderly. All business.

Emotions, on the other hand, are messy! They can really hurt our hearts. And it's human nature to avoid pain. We have centuries of this avoidance behind us. After all, do you think your great-great-grandparents had the luxury of working out their feelings? Likely they were too busy surviving. Now we even have entire spiritual systems based on emotional avoidance. I see emotions like a passionate, wild, red-haired woman crashing a formal event. She will not be denied. Better let her in and hear what she's got to say.

Most people enter this work thinking, *I'll get what I want, and then I'll be happy*. It's actually the reverse. You get happy and then what you want comes. Releasing stress and processing pain will be a part of your happiness prescription, no waiting necessary.

Emotions 101

1. **Emotions aren't (just) in your head.** The stressful narrative you're running about why you're feeling the way you're feeling is in your conscious mind. But that's not where the actual emotions are. They are in your energy field, which comprises the entire body. The emotions may rest in your knotted stomach or in that electricity running up and down your back.

2. **Talking yourself out of a feeling doesn't always work.** See #1. There are times when thoughts can neutralize emotions, but not usually. If the thoughts try in any way to negate or judge the experience, the feelings will actually intensify. For example, your coworker takes credit for your idea. You feel betrayed and angry. If you start thinking thoughts such as, *He didn't mean it. I'm probably overreacting*, you have denied the feelings. Two

weeks later, you're putting a fist into his birthday cake. Oops! The feelings didn't go away. They just waited until a weak and unguarded moment to take over.

3. **You probably never learned effective emotional processing growing up. But you can now.** This is an essential life skill. We are fortunate to be able to do these processes now. Let go of any blame for parents/caregivers/teachers. No one can teach you what they themselves didn't know. Much of what we now know about emotions is recent information.

4. **Emotions are not logical.** See #1 and #2. Once you recognize this, you can accept emotions for what they are rather than trying to debate them.

5. **Emotions are information.** They are telling you something about how you interpret the world and everything in it. Be willing to listen.

6. **Suppression (ultimately) hurts worse than feeling the feelings.** Any temporary relief from stuffing down or denying your uncomfortable feelings will be short-lived. Those feelings still exist within your energy field and body tissues. They can cause a lot of other physical and emotional problems. Isn't it better to deal with them now?

7. **All emotions are a part of one spectrum.** When you suppress your anger, anxiety, and grief, it is much more difficult to feel the positive emotions you crave—like joy, happiness, and love.

Here's how to begin a regular practice of what I call emotional alchemy:

MANIFESTING MINI PROCESS

Emotional Alchemy

1. **Start where you are.** You experience emotional highs and lows throughout the day. You'll know if a feeling needs to be processed if you continue thinking about it after the triggering event has concluded.

Example: You approach a cashier in a drugstore and offer a friendly hello. The cashier doesn't look at you or respond. You feel annoyed.

If later that evening or the next morning or a week later while complaining to a friend, you're still thinking about it, this needs to be processed.

It could be touching on something deeper. Or this incident itself just needs to be released.

If, however, you haven't given it a second thought since you left the store, there's no need to delve.

Begin a regular practice of neutralizing these negative feelings. Once a week is a great way to start.

2. **Journal.** I recommend this over and over and over again because it works. A journal is a safe place for your feelings to be unloaded without harming anyone. Bring pen to paper and keep writing until you've emptied out. Don't censor or analyze. Just regurgitate onto the page. Be as mean, vengeful, and toxic as you'd like. Keep writing until you feel empty.

For some, this exercise works better when done by audio. Using a voice memo app or other digital recording software, let it rip. Complain, yell, scream, threaten. Keep going until you feel bottomed out. *This alone can process the emotions.* You'll know they are processed if you feel better. If you don't . . .

3. **Further process the feelings.** You can do this in a number of ways, many mentioned throughout this book. And here we have:

  a. **Feel the feelings.** Feel what happens in your body when you think of this upsetting topic. Stop, be present to these sensations, and breathe into those areas where you are holding the emotion. Let the emotional energy transform.

  b. **Fire ritual.** Breathe the emotions into something flammable like a dried leaf, herb (like sage), or stick, and with intention, burn it, allowing the emotion to release.

c. **Shower cleanse.** Imagine the water in your shower is golden light and see it washing the emotion out of your body and down the drain.

4. **Get positive!** This is extremely important. After you've cleared the congested emotional energy, fill in this spaciousness you've created with the positive opposite. Arouse good thoughts and feelings using any number of ideas and practices in this book. Now that you've neutralized the pain and created space, your affirmations, visualizations, acting as if, and other practices can take root, grow, and manifest, at times so quickly that it will rock your world!

24

Dealing with Doubts and Releasing Resistance

Setting yourself up for success means preparing for pitfalls. Doubts, yours and others', are a natural part of the process. You've chosen to stop passively accepting life as you know it. You're stepping up and saying, "I want more, and I can choose to create it." That's a bold decision and an uncommon one that we don't often see reflected back to us in our social circle, the media, and popular culture. You're choosing to jump up and down out on a shaky limb. Skateboard the road less traveled. Doubts will not be far behind. Even the most optimistic and enthusiastic manifestor will encounter doubts on the journey.

> People have a hard time letting go of their suffering. Out of a fear of the unknown, they prefer suffering that is familiar.
>
> —**Thich Nhat Hanh**

There are many who will say, "Ignore the doubts. Just stay focused on the goal." That usually didn't work so well for me. When I applied this method, manifesting took a very long time, if it happened at all. I felt an inner tug-of-war between the part of me that didn't believe it could happen and the part of me that oh so wanted to believe it could. The energy of that war was an impediment to it happening. Denying an inner voice that needed to be heard just seemed to make it stronger.

When I learned to welcome and work with my inner doubter, that part of me became an ally rather than a liability.

Here are some common doubts to manifestation:

1. **"This can't happen for me."**

2. **"I'm not ready."**

3. **"The Universe/life is against me."**

4. **"What if it doesn't work?"**

5. **"It's impossible / too hard / too unlikely to happen."**

6. **"I don't know how to create this." / "I don't know how this can possibly work out."**

7. **"No one in my family (or that I know) has ever (been successful, made six figures, had a healthy relationship, etc.)."**

Some real advice for the doubts:

1. **"This can't happen for me."** You don't have what you desire now, so then it can't possibly happen in the future. Yet there was a time you were in grade school, and that's no longer the case. There were times when you were single and then times when you were not. There are times you've made less money and times you've made more. Change is always happening! Make those changes positive ones.

2. **"I'm not ready."** Leave your readiness up to the Universe. Manifestations I've seen take years to come into form did so because I had not yet become the woman who could manage them. Once I became that person, they unfolded perfectly for me. Once I got really good at managing my finances, "mysteriously" I had more money to manage. You focus on the work and leave the timing in higher hands. Affirm, "This is all unfolding in divine timing." Nothing ever happens fast enough for my taste. It's just the way I'm built. But even I've learned, how can I possibly argue with divine timing? And I'd like you to consider that you're

actually readier than you think you are. Otherwise, why would you be reading this book? Don't wait. The time is now. Always.

3. **"The Universe/life is against me."** Look for the ways you may have worked against life. Constant complaining, focusing on what's wrong, not taking personal responsibility for your life (because you didn't know how), giving the source of your happiness over to other people, and waiting for permission or approval from others to shine are all ways we work against life. And the top habits that take us away from our good? Self-criticism, self-blame, and shame. You are a beloved child of the Universe, exactly as you are. The second you condemn this beautiful creation that is you, you move against the very rhythm of existence. Develop self-love and life will work for you.

4. **"What if it doesn't work?"** This doubt is trying to protect you from disappointment. But here's the thing: If you're still breathing, how do you know the manifesting hasn't worked? It just hasn't worked *yet*. Perhaps it hasn't appeared in the form you expected. But the Universe has an infinite number of resources at its disposal. Time and time again, just when I think there is no other way, a way is made, and it's always better than what I had planned. When this doubt creeps in, make sure to utilize the word *yet*. "This hasn't worked *yet*. I am open to it unfolding perfectly now."

5. **"It's impossible / too hard / too unlikely to happen."** If this is your most prevalent doubt, you are the reality checkers. Forever comparing what could be against what is, you are the statistic checkers and fact collectors. "Last year unemployment for women over sixty rose by 29 percent. There's no way I can find a good job." As someone with a degree in sociology who also happens to love statistics, let me share that stats don't mean much. First off, they are based on incomplete samples. Unless every single person in the country or on the earth has been polled, they are making educated guesses based on limited data. And haven't we seen in recent political polls of all types just how far off they can be? And I also want to say, so what? Yes, so what if unemployment rose in your demographic? It does not mean *you* can't find or create a fulfilling job.

6. **"I don't know how to create this." / "I don't know how this can possibly work out."** Just like the timing, the *how* is not up to you. It is beyond your pay grade. Sorry, not sorry. You will never be able to adopt a bird's-eye view of all the moving parts and how they relate to their other surrounding moving parts. That's good news for all of us. If we did know, our humanness could really screw it up with its endless agendas. You can admit, "I don't see how this can happen," and then follow it with, "And I don't need to know. I give this fully and freely over to the all-knowing, all-powerful Universe and allow it to perfectly take form now."

7. **"No one in my family (or that I know) has ever (been successful, made six figures, had a healthy relationship, etc.)."** Maybe no one you know has, but someone somewhere certainly has. Immerse yourself in true stories of those who have created what you'd like to have. Get to know them and learn about their successes. This lets both the conscious and subconscious mind know this is possible. Also, think of something else you've done or experienced that no one else you know has. Maybe you were the first to graduate from college or the first to travel to another country. If you did that, you can do this!

Manifesting Reflection Journaling on Doubts

1. **Imagine your manifestation in great detail.** If the doubts aren't organically coming into awareness, ask the Universe to show them to you. Write them down. Include any above that resonate.

2. **One at time, explore them, emptying all the "supporting evidence" for them onto the page.**

3. **Now go deeper.** Inquire. Ask, "This can't happen because . . ." and fill in the blanks with all possible answers. Examples:

    This can't happen because . . .

    I never finished college.

    I'm not a scholar.

Nothing has ever worked out for me.

I'm too old/tired/fat/stupid/lazy, etc.

I'm cursed.

Flush out the "reasons."

4. **Do one of the processes on pages 202–209.**

Resistance

The difference between doubts and resistance is that doubts are conscious. You hear them in your head. And they can be reflected back to you by the people in your life. You know exactly what they are. Our relationship with resistance, I can honestly say, well, "It's complicated."

Resistance is normally unconscious. It masquerades as excuses, procrastination, and unhealthy habits. But lurking beneath these energy zappers is a deep resistance to change. The possibility of positive change will bring resistance to the surface quickly. Exposing the dark mold of resistance to the sun and air of awareness helps dry it up.

My client Valerie has dreams of becoming a movie scriptwriter. Having written two plays while still in high school, she majored in literature and, postcollege, landed a job in publishing. Her days became filled with reading other people's writing. Often, a voice in her head said, *You could have written that! You're better than this.* Movies, with their predictable plotlines and trite dialogue, frustrated her. This is an area she could shine; she was sure of it. She decided to write for one hour each evening after dinner but found herself too tired to be inspired. How about getting up an hour earlier to write? she thought. This well-intentioned solution lasted for all of four days. Suddenly, she began staying up much later than usual, watching movies until 2:00 a.m., unable to turn off the remote.

> Pain is a relatively objective, physical phenomenon; suffering is our psychological resistance to what happens. Events may create physical pain, but they do not in themselves create suffering. Resistance creates suffering. Stress happens when your mind resists what is . . . The only problem in your life is your mind's resistance to life as it unfolds.
>
> —Dan Millman

Her mornings a washout, she was barely getting to work on time. Let alone writing. Valerie had encountered resistance and did not know what to do about it.

I used a technique with Valerie called *tapping* to bust through her resistance. (See page 202 for instructions.) The normal excuses came up. "I work so hard. I want to watch movies at night. It's my only relaxation. Don't I deserve to enjoy something I really love?" But as we continued to tap, what came up was a fear of failure. Here she had spent years telling herself how much better she was than the authors she worked with. What if she had been wrong all along?

As we tapped, I asked her, "If you failed, what's the worst that could happen?" She spit out a long list of terrible, but extremely unlikely, possibilities. Everything from "All my friends will leave me" to "I'll have nothing to live for." As we continued tapping, more likely scenarios presented themselves. "It will be all my fault. I had a gift and I ignored it," and "I'm such an egomaniac! Who am I to judge any working writer?" Once we neutralized all these thoughts, Valerie was able to forgive herself. She realized her jealousy had been a painful gift. It was telling her, "You have a talent, but don't believe you can be successful at it." That's what jealousy says to us all. "I want that, but I don't believe I can have it, so I'm bitter about the person who does." The problem is jealousy feels so painful, we often turn away from the gift. Neutralize the doubt in your ability to have what you want, and the jealousy disappears. Often those people you are jealous of can be way-showers. They are living examples of what is possible and may have a blueprint, tips, or simply hope to assist you on your journey.

Manifesting Resistance Busters: Tapping

Tapping is a term used to describe methods of using the fingers to rhythmically tap on the meridian points used in acupuncture. The theory is doubts and fears are actual blockages in our energy field. Once these blockages are released, doubts disappear and fears vanish. Tapping releases those blocks. It's also a bridge to the subconscious mind, so it's ideal for revealing hidden causes behind destructive behaviors. Like in the example with Valerie, for anything unknown, I would start here.

This is a highly simplified version of Emotional Freedom Techniques (EFT), the original and most popular form of tapping. If you enjoy tapping and want to go deeper, my book *Energy Healing* contains a detailed primer to get you started, along with several other simple transformative and balancing exercises.

Meridian Points Used

Under the Eye: Using both hands, tap on the face underneath each eye, on the cheekbones.

Collarbone: Using both hands, tap underneath both sides of the collarbones, on the upper chest.

Thymus: Using both hands, alternating Tarzan-style, tap on the hard breastbone in the center of the chest.

Instructions

1. Using your fingertips, begin tapping under each eye, on the collarbone points, and on the thymus, alternating back and forth in whatever intervals feel right for you.

2. Bring the doubt to mind and see how strongly you believe it. 1 being it's barely believable to 10 meaning it feels 100 percent true to you.

3. As you tap through the points, go into the negativity and describe the doubt, all the reasons for it, why it can never happen.

4. Keep tapping until the belief feels neutral or no longer true.

5. Create affirmations that are the positive opposite of the doubt and tap those in. (For suggestions, see Manifesting Alchemy Practice 1: Affirmations and Scripting along with other affirmations used throughout the book.)

Manifesting Resistance Busters: Brief Energy Correction

I learned this from my colleague, renowned psychologist and energy psychology pioneer Robin Bilazarian. It's called a *Brief Energy Correction*, and it quickly reduces the emotional intensity of just about everything, including doubts and resistance.

Meridian Points Used

Points around the belly button. These are accessed by laying a flat hand against the abdomen with the belly button under the center of the palm. This hand remains still while the other hand is used to hold on to the following points:

Collarbone as used in tapping exercise on page 203.

Under the nose and above the upper lip.

On the chin

On the tailbone

Instructions

1. Think of a doubt or a behavior of resistance. Drop into your body. What do you feel when you focus on this? Scan the body for areas of discomfort.

2. Rate the discomfort on a scale from 1 to 10.

3. Place your nondominant hand on your abdomen. Leave it there while you touch and hold the other points.

4. With your dominant hand, place it on the upper chest, on top of the collarbone, under the neck.

5. Take a deep breath in through the nose and out through the mouth.

6. Bring the fingers of your dominant hand under the nose and hold.

7. Take a deep breath in through the nose and out through the mouth.

8. Bring the fingers of your dominant hand to your chin and hold.

9. Take a deep breath in through the nose and out through the mouth.

10. Now bring the dominant hand around your back and place it on the tailbone at the base of the spine.

11. Take a deep breath in through the nose and out through the mouth.

12. Bring the dominant hand back to the collarbone.

13. Repeat this process in four to ten cycles until the intensity is greatly reduced.

14. Place one hand on top of the other in the center of the chest. Taking a deep breath in, affirm: "It is safe to have and be more."

Manifesting Resistance Busters: Smashing the Egg of Resistance

Based on a qigong practice I learned decades ago, this simplified version may look ridiculous to outside observers but it truly works. The feeling of freedom after release provides much relief from old baggage.

1. Purchase a dozen eggs, or more, if you're really struggling. Buy these specifically for the ritual rather than grabbing a few from the ones you eat.

2. Find a private setting in nature. If you have pine trees in your local area, go for those. Otherwise, any trees will do.

3. Take one egg out and hold it in your hand.

4. Think of one doubt or one habit of resistance. Get in touch with the energy of it.

5. Bring the egg up close to your face and imagine you are blowing the doubt and all the painful energy into it.

6. Let it rip. Pull your arm back and throw it against the tree so it smashes. (If you've got bad aim, get close to the tree.)

7. Feel the relief that follows.

8. Affirm: "This is done. This is over. This is gone. I am free!"

This exercise is a perfect example of my resiliency. The first time I tried this, I went into a small public park, late at night, so it would be deserted. The perimeter of the park is where I found the trees, and this was surrounded by suburban houses on all sides. I began doing the exercise, quietly, I promise you. The outside lights came on at the house directly across the street. Not long after, I saw a police car approaching in the distance, and I leaped arms-first into a thorny bush! The police pulled up in front of the house and the homeowners came out, speaking of "suspicious pranks" by "teenagers." (For the record, I was thirty-four and acted alone.) The police patrolled the area for twenty minutes, and when they finally left, I pulled myself out, muddied, bloodied, and utterly humiliated. You do get a few scrapes on a spiritual path! To this day, I don't know why I didn't just fess up. But can you imagine the conversation? "Gee, Officers, I'm doing this process to release deeply held doubts, based on ancient qigong practices. I'm so broke and spent my last two bucks on these eggs to manifest more money. So I was blowing the doubts into these eggs, see, and I had to find trees to throw them at . . ." Let's face it, I was dressed in black, carrying raw eggs, and would have been spouting this story? I'd still be locked up!

This is a good time to remind you to be conscious and cautious about with whom you share your manifesting journey. The haters are not safe places for sprinkling your fairy dust of enthusiasm and grand plans. And I'm thinking law enforcement isn't likely the most open-minded source as well. Save yourself some trouble and find a hidden spot for all outdoor activities.

Manifesting Resistance Busters: Shattering Doubts

This is a similar exercise to the egg one but uses glass instead. Get yourself a set of safety goggles for this one.

1. Find glass you're okay breaking. Green glass is particularly good for releasing frustrating doubts, so mineral water or beer bottles are ideal, just remove the labels. Feel free to get creative here. If you're breaking long-held family doubts, your grandmother's ugly pitcher may be an ideal sacrifice. Still using your married dishes and you're long divorced? Buh-bye. Time to get cracking on those.

2. Find an ideal setting here. Of course, I do not recommend leaving broken glass in nature or anywhere it can be harmful or annoying to others. An abandoned factory? Or a no-longer-used train yard? These could work. If you don't live near such gritty Guy Ritchie

cinematic settings, then do this at home. A metal garbage can also work well. If you let it double as your recycling container, it saves you a step.

3. Choose your vessel. Think of one doubt or one habit of resistance. Get in touch with the energy of it.

4. Blow on it or yell it into the vessel.

5. Now for the fun part. Smash it to bits! Throw it. Smash it with a hammer or a rock. Let it rip!

6. Feel the relief that follows.

7. Affirm: "This is done. This is over. This is gone. I am free!"

If you're cleaning up shards, be sure to do this safely, with gloves.

Manifesting Resistance Busters: Dancing on the Ashes

Burning prayers, burdens, and divine requests has been done for thousands of years. Ancient peoples believed the smoke carried these communications to heaven. For me, heaven is above me, below me, all around me, and within me. Fire is an element of transformation that allows those inner burdens to be dissolved, creating spaciousness for the new.

1. Find a fireproof container. A large, heavy-bottomed stainless steel or cast-iron cooking pot with a lid works.

2. If you're in an apartment, do this over the stove with the exhaust fan on or find a private place out in nature. Avoid fire alarms and overhead sprinklers! House dwellers can use a fire pit in the backyard.

3. On a small piece of paper, write out a single doubt and supporting information. Continue with all the other doubts, each on its own paper.

4. Hold each paper and say a little prayer of release. It could sound like, "Oh, Universe, I am ready to let this go and be free."

5. Light a match or use a lighter or stove or fire from the pit and ignite the paper, quickly dropping it in the fireproof container.

6. Repeat for each paper.

7. Sprinkle the ashes on the ground, turn on some uplifting music, and literally dance on them as you crush them into the ground.

8. Affirm: "I give these ashes and any remaining remnants back to you, sweet Universe. I am free."

Notice that with all these exercises, I ended them with an affirmation. The ones included here are merely suggestions, and I encourage you to create and use your own. Get specific. What is the positive opposite of the belief or resistance you've just released?

Here are some additional affirmations for the common doubts to manifestation:

1. **"This can't happen for me."**

   "Everything is going my way."

   "I am worthy of all the good life has to offer."

2. **"I'm not ready."**

   "I am ready to embrace my true place in life."

   "I am ready to embrace positive change."

3. **"The Universe/life is against me."**

   "The Universe is conspiring in my favor."

   "The Universe loves me."

4. **"What if it doesn't work?"**

   "I am open to everything working perfectly for me now."

   "This has worked for others, and it now works for me."

5. **"It's impossible / too hard / too unlikely to happen."**

   "The Universe is all knowing and all powerful and is creating this for me now."

"Everything is possible."

There's a quote from the Bible that you can use if it resonates: "With God all things are possible."

6. **"I don't know how to create this." / "I don't know how this can possibly work out."**

"Everything I need to know, I know. Everything I need to do, I do, easily and joyously."

> Inaction breeds doubt and fear. Action breeds confidence and courage. If you want to conquer fear, do not sit home and think about it. Go out and get busy.
>
> **—Dale Carnegie**

"I leave the how to the Universe. It knows exactly what to do."

"I let go completely and trust that it is working out perfectly now."

7. **"No one in my family (that I know of) has ever (been successful, made six figures, had a healthy relationship, etc)."**

"It is safe and good to be the first in my family to create *this*." (Use your specific goal)

"My ancestral lineage was built on many firsts, and I am following in that tradition."

"I researched real life examples of people who have created this. They did it and I am doing it now too."

"If it's possible for anyone to _____ (ex. make six figures), then it's definitely possible for me."

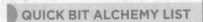

QUICK BIT ALCHEMY LIST

5 Ways You Hold Yourself Back (and Probably Don't Realize It)

1. **Negative self-talk**
   Making this change alone will create positivity in every area of your life.

2. **Clutter**
   Clutter is stuck energy. Clear it and new opportunities (and money) can come in.

3. **Stinginess**
   Tip well and often. Pick up the check. Purchase the nicer gift. Give with a full heart.

4. **Blaming and shaming**
   Stop searching for the outrage du jour to bitch about on Twitter. You ain't changing anyone's ideas, believe me. Look out for people who are actively making the world better.

5. **Not forgiving**
   Forgiveness isn't condoning. It's freeing yourself from continuing to be at the mercy of other people's behavior. Take back your power now.

25

Opposites Attracted

NOW WHAT?
A.K.A. THE OTHER SHOE HAS DROPPED

This is not what you thought would happen.

You've been visualizing bundles of cash in your accounts.

Your plumbing springs a serious leak amounting to $8,000 in repairs.

You've vision-boarded your dream wedding down to the perfect napkins.

Your fiancée ends the engagement.

Listing every quality you want in the perfect career, you reread it religiously.

You get fired.

"Everything fell apart! That wasn't supposed to happen!" It can. Not always. But it can indeed happen. You didn't do anything

> An arrow can only be shot by pulling it backward. So when life is dragging you back with difficulties, it means that it's going to launch you into something great. So just focus and keep aiming.
>
> **—Paulo Coelho**

wrong. In fact, this actually means you're doing a very effective manifesting job.

"How can you say that? This isn't what I wanted!"

How I can say this is experience, my dear Conscious Cocreators, experience. You're stirring up your energy. Going against prevailing patterns. Opening the door for more. There are times when what is must crumble to create room for the new.

Our lives, finances, jobs, and relationships can be built on unsolid ground. They can be built on unworthiness. Or a belief that "I can't have what I want." Or "Nothing ever works out for me." The cracks in the foundation either need to be fixed or swapped out for an entirely new platform. Change can be swift. The foundation crumbles underneath you and you're left wondering what went wrong.

Here's what to do:

1. **Acknowledge and process the feelings.** See chapters 23 and 24, "The Power of Emotion" and "Dealing with Doubts and Releasing Resistance."

2. **Move into accepting what is.** The plumbing still needs to be fixed. The wedding "save the date" scrapped. Get Big S Support (the Universe) first, then call on small s support (friends and family) and begin taking action.

   A few helpful prayers for this:

   "Great Universe, I feel so lost. I need help now!"

   "I don't know why this happened, Universe, so I am giving it all over to You. Please show me guidance and support."

   "Guide me, oh Universe, to resolution and peace. I need You."

3. **Please remember: it's darkest before the dawn.** Normally, on the other side of "Opposites Attracted" are quantum leaps forward. Hang on!

4. **Commands of denial.** Unlike the unconscious kind of denial, this one is an out-loud refusal. You're accessing your inner authority. Here are a few options to get you started.

"I am not limited by this! This situation has no power over me. I take my true place with my true prosperity and with my true people now."

"Nothing can limit my good! No, not even this! I let go and trust that all I need and desire is mine now."

"I release this situation entirely. I let it go. In faith, I know good is manifesting perfectly for me now."

5. **Return to your manifestation process. Focus.** Continue with what you were doing or switch to another process, keeping the same outcomes in mind. When your mind gets distracted by the current circumstances, bring it back to focusing on what you want.

6. **Keep going!** Persistence is key. As I mentioned, "Opposites Attracted" is a good sign. Keep moving forward. Don't give up a minute before the manifestation is due to arrive.

26

What to Do If It's Not Working (Yet)

Whatever you do, don't give up! Anything but that will help to keep your momentum moving forward. The creative process is just that: a process. More than anyone, I wish it were a straight, predictable, clean line. It just never has been. You think you got an intuitive insight that led to a dead end. The dream position came with a demanding new boss. You return to the practices, refine, tweak, and get clearer and clearer as you go along. There will always be something to work on.

Rather than approaching manifestation like a single experiment to achieve a goal, embrace this as a new way of living. Make your life your art. You are creating anyway. Doing it consciously is much more satisfying!

Here are practices to get you through the blocks.

Manifesting Reflection Journaling on "What Must I Become?"

Think of what you're manifesting.

1. **What qualities does a person who has this possess?** Create affirmations that contain those qualities.

   "I am fully confident in myself and my abilities."

   "I am intelligent and have valuable ideas."

   "I am fortunate. Everything is going my way."

   "I am likable and attract the right people to help propel me forward."

   "I am courageous and strong."

2. **What habits would a person with those qualities have?** Create affirmations that contain those habits.

   "I wake up early, excited to focus on my goals."

   "I believe in myself and my ability to create what I desire."

   "It's easy to stay focused on my goals."

   "I am making time for my dreams."

3. **Acting as if.** Begin embodying those qualities and habits. When you come up against a familiar challenge, instead of your normal reaction, stop and ask yourself:

   "What would a wealthy person do here?" or

   "How would someone who knows their beauty and worth respond here?"

   See Manifesting Alchemy Practice 6: Acting As If for more information.

Loosen the Grip

There are times when we simply hold too tightly to a dream. The stronger we squeeze, try to control, and make it happen, the less manifesting works. This usually happens with "the biggies," those things we want more than anything. Longing can be excruciating.

Longing is actually two emotions in one. There is the purity of the desire, which feels delicious and glorious. Ever feel steeped in desire prior to a romantic rendezvous? Those feelings are intoxicating. And if your paramour didn't show up, there's the "not having" this desire, which feels awful. It's important to separate the "not having" from the desire itself. When you're in the purity of the desire without pain, it can materialize in your reality.

1. **Neutralize: "I can't have this because . . ."** Use the tapping process on page 203.

   Tap while saying out loud, "I can't have this because _____." Begin with the first reason you believe this can't happen. If it brings up emotion, keep tapping until it feels neutral. Then return to the phrase "I can't have this because _____." Fill in the blank with the next reason. Keep going until you've worked through the obvious ones and some unexpected "evidence" begins popping up. Make sure to tap repeatedly on each reason that contains an emotional charge until it feels neutral before going on to the next one. Remember, emotions aren't logical. You may find yourself saying something like, "I can't have this because . . . I'm a bad girl." You think, "What does that mean?!" It's just old programming. Accept and allow whatever comes up. Then neutralize.

2. **Raise the percentages of believability.** After you've reduced the reasons for not having, now raise the percentages of what is believable for you. Rather than engage with logic, you're going to work with the subconscious mind using a symbol.

   In percentages, how believable is this outcome for you?

   In your mind, see a gauge or thermometer with the numbers 0 through 100.

   Each day, close your eyes and imagine the percentage of believability rising until it has reached 100 percent.

3. **Reignite the desire.** Imagine it in great detail. Savor it. Get excited for its arrival.

4. **Open the outcome.** Your desired outcome may be too rigid. Let go of the specifics, and focus on the feelings you believe

this manifestation will give you. Focus on just feeling good in the present moment with your life and its gifts. Engage in entertainment that makes you feel good.

5. **Give over.** I said, "Don't give up!" But by all means, do give over. If your part feels complete, then it's time to surrender. Revisit Manifesting Alchemy Principle 7: Surrender and Control.

10 Ways to Sabotage Your Success

1. **Procrastinate.**
   Manifestations have a flow. When we put off the action steps needed to bring goals to fruition, we halt that flow.

2. **Don't ask for help.**
   We can't accomplish our dreams all on our own. Don't let pride keep you from getting wisdom, advice, and skills from others.

3. **Start but don't finish.**
   Incomplete projects means stuck, stifled energy.

4. **Eat the wrong foods.**
   You may have noticed that when you eat nuts, it makes your stomach hurt, or that dairy gives you a headache. If you find yourself craving and consuming foods that make you feel bad, you're in sabotage mode.

5. **Gossip.**
   Spreading bad news, sharing private information, and even silently taking pleasure in another's misfortune gets in the way of you receiving your good.

6. **Consume negative entertainment.**
   You'll know it's negative by how it makes you feel. If a song, movie, or TV show makes you feel helpless, frightened, or angry, especially after it's over, you're cultivating sabotage.

7. **Share too much with the wrong people.**
   Letting others know what you're planning to create, especially the naysayers in your life, can easily throw you off.

8. **Waste time.**
   We have endless ways to idle away precious hours, especially on our phones. We each get twenty-four hours in a day. Wasting time depletes your creative energy.

9. **Give up.**
   You get started and hit the first roadblock, giving up before manifestation can occur.

10. **Ignore your intuition.**
    There is a portal of advice and answers inside you, but the responses aren't always logical. Talk yourself out of this inner wisdom at your own peril.

Putting It All Together

You've encountered all this book has to offer: principles, stories, insights, and practices. Lots and lots of practices! Ones for your mind, emotions, body, spirit, and energy. This way you can approach manifesting from every conceivable angle, using all the levels and dimensions of your being. Some require very little but an open mind and a bit of time. Others involve more delving and effort. Please don't be overwhelmed. You're learning not just new exercises but a different way of being.

> You must master a new way to think before you can master a new way to be.
>
> **—Marianne Williamson**

Here are some reminders and a format that can work well:

1. **Start small.** Even though I've manifested for many years, I still like to remind and reinforce what is possible for myself. I do this by manifesting the parking spot, the best appointment time, the perfect concert buddy. Regularly, I am flexing my manifesting muscles.

2. **Choose one area to work on at a time.** Please trust me on this one. I stubbornly would try to manifest in several areas at once, usually with dismal results. When you first learn to manifest, it

can feel like being that kid in the candy store. "I want this! And I want that!" You do not want to turn into Veruca Salt from the film *Willy Wonka & the Chocolate Factory*. That was the spoiled little girl who wanted the golden-egg-laying goose. "I want it all, Daddy, and I want it now!" When you've been experiencing lack for a long time, this is a natural side effect. You want your bigger life, and yesterday! Just remember, you'll never get it all done. This isn't an assignment to be turned in by a specific date. This is a new lifestyle. And you'll accomplish much more, in a shorter period of time, if your energy is focused on one manifestation at a time.

3. **Explore the practices you'd love to do and the ones that scare you.** If an exercise in the book brings up strong feelings, both positive and negative, then start with those. The positive ones will be easy. There's something already attractive about them that you're responding to. But what about the negative ones? The ones you really, really don't want to do? Those are sparking up your resistance to change. That's where the gold is. Certainly, embark on those. And the ones that make you go *eh*? Forget them for now. They just don't resonate at this time. With books like these, you can return again and again. And those "eh practices" may feel right at a later time.

4. **Set aside manifesting time.** Find the right time of day or the perfect day of the week, and put manifesting time on your calendar. When you actually schedule personal growth time, you're sending a signal to your subconscious and the Universe that you mean business! Block out distractions and minimize interruptions. Unless you're using your smartphone as a part of your manifesting process, turn it off. Make manifesting an enjoyable experience you look forward to, rather than another item on your to-do list. You've decided to become more of what your soul came here to be. You're forgetting the status quo and becoming a Conscious Creator. This is exciting! Light a candle. Play soft, relaxing, meditative music in the background. Make this time an oasis you're happy to come into.

5. **Get support.** Enlist the support of a fellow manifestor or accountability partner. Form a mastermind group or book club

group so you have folks to share in the adventure and keep you motivated.

Form a group that is working toward specific goals and mutually support one another with ideas, brainstorming, accountability, and spiritual practices.

6. **Find good whenever you can find it.** It really is all around us.

7. **Make emotional journey practices a part of your life.** You have an emotional body. When it's honored, cleared, and balanced, it's your greatest asset.

8. **Make manifestation a part of your everyday life.** Once practiced, many of these principles can be integrated into your everyday life. Find the gaps when you'd otherwise be wasting time, and make it manifestation time.

> I am knowing great love, abundance, and success for you.

> I am knowing all of you are developing the most incredible connections you could ever experience, with your True Self and with the Universe, and that these relationships nourish, guide, and delight you.

> I am knowing you release struggle and embrace ease.

> I am knowing you are emerging out of old ideas about yourself to be more of who you came into this life to be.

> I am knowing you're falling more deeply in love with your everyday existence and the people in it, including yourself.

> There is nothing sweeter!

QUICK BIT ALCHEMY LIST

5 Powerful Ways to End Your Day

1. Write a couple of brief sentences about anything that bothered you. Circle them all and put a slash through it.

2. Put a hand across your forehead and breathe deeply, saying, "I let this day go."

3. Imagine breathing in and out through the center of the chest for two minutes. Write down something you're grateful for. Describe in scintillating details that arouse warm, loving feelings.

4. Imagine golden light emanating out from the chest and gently encompassing your whole being, bringing lightness and peace.

5. Pray. Affirm. Ask. And know you are heard, known, and loved.

Conclusion

As I'm completing this manuscript, the spring of 2020 is giving way to summer. And by "completing," in true ADD fashion, I actually mean, "writing the majority of." This winter saw the arrival of the COVID-19 coronavirus, and everyday life around the globe has been upended, bringing people everywhere face-to-face with painful fears. There's been significant loss, and most everyone is struggling with how to keep moving forward with nothing but uncertainty meeting them each day.

Others are getting clear about what's most important to them, going within, taking time for renewal, learning more about themselves and the people closest to them, reevaluating their truest values and using the downtime to appreciate all that they have. There's a massive wake-up call happening.

My experience has been unique.

Overnight, as news of the virus broke, I experienced a synching up, a clicking in, into an alignment with a Power Greater Than Myself. It was like the Universe was tapping me on the shoulder and pulling me into the game. In my mind, the Universe took the form of gravel-voiced Mickey, the boxing coach for Rocky, from the famous movie. "Get in there, kid! They need ya!" A powerful surge of energy saturated my entire being, and I was bounding out of bed each morning, ready to don my superhero cape and get to work. Instantaneously, my private practice quadrupled. A lot of the one-on-one work I do is with folks with crippling anxiety. Suddenly, we had all been dropped into the Super Bowl of anxiety, and I was going for Most Valuable Player. I had a singular, all-pervasive focus: serve absolutely everyone I possibly could. Clients peeled through layers of past wounds faster than ever before. Core issues rose to the surface and were cleared. I know an enormous amount about creating emotional relief, and now was the time to share these skills in a bigger way. I offered a free online group energy healing, and a hundred people attended. So I turned this into a weekly event that lasted nine weeks. My writing shifted from this book to my newsletter, offering weekly doses of comfort, compassion, and stress-relieving practices to help navigate this confusing terrain. For almost six weeks, I worked six and a half days a week, from twelve to eighteen hours per day, and somehow managed to shop, cook, do laundry, and walk in nature as much as I could. Nature offered moments of absolute bliss. I experienced more clearly than I ever had before: I am one with everything. (We *all* are one with everything.) One with the towering trees. One with flowering cherry blossoms. One with the droplets of rain. One with the reflection of light dancing across the pond. Everything felt both more mysterious and yet clearer than ever before. If only people knew they could get this high organically! The oddest aspect of it all was my sense of humor became heightened to the point of the absurd. I shared funny memes and texted jokes to anyone who could stand me. I acted like a bit of a smart-ass in the chat feature under our governor's daily briefings. His sign language interpreter was a handsome man. Among everyone's complaints, I would disperse a funny comment here and there, like, "Is it wrong that I wish he were signing with his shirt off?" or "It would be hard to stay six feet from him!" It made people laugh when laughter was in short supply. I felt compelled to add just a little bit of levity in all the seriousness, adopting a new role, the holy fool. Dancing to the overhead music in grocery stores while I scanned the ransacked shelves, there were moments when I would look around at the bewildered reactions of other shoppers. One woman barked through her mask, "What the f— are you so happy about?!" I wish I'd had an answer for her. But I know from experience, supernatural experiences are ones to be lived now and examined later. And often that examination is futile. I didn't know why this was happening to me, I just knew it was meant to happen. My humanness had been relegated to the back seat by my spirit. I could occasionally hear Human Kris softly in the background, eking out concerns. "Do we have enough toilet paper? What if there are food shortages? We are so alone." Super Spirit Kris heard her. Listened. Met her with compassion. Then didn't let it slow her down for one second. I was on a mission. And I felt a greater trust in the Universe than ever before. I felt protected, guided, and very much loved.

You can imagine that this was difficult to explain to family and friends. Everyone was scrambling to make sense of what was happening, forming opinions, and doing everything in their power to feel safe. The people in my life ran the gamut on responses, from those who hadn't left their homes in months to the virus deniers refusing to wear masks, with every possible variation in between. Miraculously, surprisingly, I was in complete non-judgment of them all. After all, I didn't know any of the answers myself, just what was mine to do. I wanted everyone to feel safe. I respected whatever choices they made that enabled them to feel that way. And I prayed for safety for humanity as a whole. That if there are lessons to be learned, we are learning them in the gentlest ways possible. It was one of many confirmations of just what a profound spiritual experience this was. Human Kris can be quite judgy, even, admittedly, a tad self-righteous at times. But Super Spirit Kris sees only love. Super Spirit Kris knows we are all doing the best we can. Super Spirit Kris allows herself to be used for the greater good. And yet just because I was feeling that way toward others, it didn't mean everyone was able to return this sentiment in kind.

Not everyone will be okay with you being okay when they're not okay. That can happen on this Magical Mystery Manifestation Mission. You are stepping back from an accepted status quo reality, taking control of your consciousness, and making life work for you as you learn to work with life. You are becoming an Alchemist. Be prepared that not everyone will be thrilled with this. Yet the best way you can help others and the world is to become a master manifestor anyway. This gives you resources to share. And not just resources but the knowledge that they too can create a life of more. More love, more money, more health, more joy. It's available for every one of us.

You can become okay with others not being okay with you.

Not immediately, but in time, you will become comfortable with a new normal. And all the benefits will keep you moving forward even when facing criticism from people you love.

After about six weeks, my supernatural experience came crashing down into the same humanness everyone else was experiencing. I had bouts of uncertainty, confusion, and an aching loneliness that I couldn't quite shake. Along with it, I began grieving for that supernatural experience. After all, who doesn't want to have boundless energy, enthusiasm, love, and faith in the face of terror? I just wasn't ready to let it go. I wanted to feel that way all the time. And yet, even during that time of questioning, my needs were covered.

My point in sharing this story is very important. Even during a world-wide pandemic, economic collapse, and terrifying riots, when everything felt wrong and nothing felt right, I was and am okay. And often, a whole lot more than okay. I did fulfilling work and expressed my creativity in writing and photos, all while I expanded my business. And here I am, now completing this book. Summer of 2020 has now given way to autumn as I complete my revisions. The leaves are beginning to change, and many of us are wondering when the constant changes we've endured will come to a stop. I miss teaching in person and traveling. And I am still okay. Most days, I am still way more than just okay. There is some modicum of what I have come to call *financial survivor's guilt* to process. Along with session fees and group donations, unexpected gifts and money have shown up in my life during a time when many people are suffering. No man or woman is an island. What good is my bounty when so many around me are in financial chaos? I've given and donated more than ever before. And the entire time, I am knowing: we all inherently have the power within us to create a whole new world here. One that works for everyone. One in which all people are safe, healthy, prosperous, happy, and free. This may be the darkness before the dawn, and I am envisioning that dawn. I hope you all will join me in that.

Here lies this book. I've provided a road map to not only actively create what you want but to cultivate an inner place of trust and safety in the Universe. Am I actually saying this information could change the world? Yes, I am saying just that. These are the principles that have been creating each stage of evolution since the dawn of time. As you can change yourself and your life, so too you can have a tremendous effect on the world.

Throughout this difficult time, besides daily energy work and prayer, I have returned to using these very tools. And I want you to know that I have been given everything I need. Absolutely. Everything.

A few examples:

After a long day of writing, I realized my refrigerator was empty. I had to choose between a much-needed walk so my body didn't atrophy or get food to make a quality dinner. My sad handful of broken plantain chips and can of tuna weren't exactly calling to me. My across-the-hall neighbor, Marc, texted. "I'm making homemade turkey soup. Would you like some?" Did I ever! After my walk, I arrived home to find a complete meal carefully arranged on a paper towel on my doormat. There was a beautiful postcard propped beside it. The message said, "We're so glad you're our neighbor." The food was delicious, healthy, filling, and fulfilling, and I ingested the energy of kindness and generosity infused in each bite.

A few years ago, I had purchased metal angel wings from an arts-and-crafts store. During COVID quarantine, I wanted to continue to support them as a customer. On a whim, I checked out the store's website, hoping to find other angel wing products, but their stock was low and the left-overs didn't appeal to me. The next day, my friend Ki'Mani offered to bring me an herbal bath she'd concocted, along with yummy homemade food. I met her outside, standing back from her car so we could catch up while socially distanced, when the sun illuminated something in her back seat. "Are those metal angel wings?" I asked.

"Yes! Do you want them?" she replied.

Pulling them out, I was stunned at how beautiful and enormous they were. She had purchased them months before, and they didn't fit in her space. I was surprised to find the tags on the wings were from the same store I had been perusing.

On a particularly lonely day when I was feeling exhausted and more than a little sorry for myself, I left my urban dwelling for my daily nature escape. Humanness was in charge that day. I had been working so hard and suddenly felt like I wanted this to be witnessed by somebody, anybody. I just needed an "attagirl" pat on the back. Stopping at the mailbox, there were two cards. One had come all the way from Holland. My dearest friend Veronique had included a package of brightly colored tissue paper Easter eggs. My eyes lit up as if they were Fabergé eggs! She said, "In these very difficult times, you are a beacon of light! Please know, I love you so very much." I exploded with tears. It was exactly what I needed to hear, exactly when I needed to hear it. Even though it had taken two weeks, this card had arrived exactly on time. The other was from my sweet friend Regina, an exceptional massage therapist who'd had to place her practice on hold due to coronavirus quarantine. She shared, "I want to let you know how special you are. I admire your willingness and open heart to provide your deeply effective online healing sessions during this tumultuous time." In thankfulness, she offered me three massages! On my walk, all I could do was weep. I felt loved. Seen. Appreciated. All whining had disappeared in an instant, replaced by gratitude. I wasn't alone after all.

I got a text from Venmo. A generous and beloved client sent me a large sum of money. I assumed it was for future session fees. Instead, it was an appreciation of gratitude for the work I had done with her and her family. As she explained this, I burst into tears. This "tip" allowed me to take a bit of much-needed time off for writing this book.

Then there were countless other generosities. My friend Mary Kay sewed four very pretty masks for me from sugar-skull-themed fabric, which get compliments every time I wear one. Then she dropped off a package of paper plates when on social media, I had offered up my mother in exchange for some! Again, another joke from the holy fool. I was just so tired of doing dishes all the time! Gorgeous original art arrived from my friends Sylvia and Desiree. Much-needed neck and shoulder support came in a luxurious aromatherapy wrap from Shaina. But wait, there's more! A slew of books. (And I *love* books!) More delicious homemade food. Lots of other greeting cards. An antique typewriter for my collection. Hilarious texts. A deepening friendship with a former acquaintance. Factor in super sweet emails from happy clients and readers of my first book, and you can see why I felt so supported at a time when it was desperately needed.

> Do not be dismayed by the brokenness of the world. All things break. And all things can be mended. Not with time, as they say, but with intention. So go. Love intentionally, extravagantly, unconditionally. The broken world waits in darkness for the light that is you.
>
> —L. R. Knost

All of it allowed me to serve from fullness, filled with grace. It wasn't that I was in denial of what was happening. I lost someone I knew personally. Three friends lost parents. My hospice volunteer mother said goodbye to two dear colleagues. Some of my favorite local businesses will likely not reopen. All my speaking and teaching gigs have been canceled, including my weekly energy sessions with blind and visually impaired students. I miss them so much! Like everyone, there's a lot I am missing. And events happening right now have left my friends of color and parents of children of color reeling. For me, being a spiritual being doesn't mean living in an alternate reality bubble. It does mean that as I take in reality, I respond with compassion and understanding, for my own reactions and for where others are. I do all that I can to be a source of love, including loving and being tender with myself. Then the more I am able to be that for others. I focus on imagining a world that works for everyone. What that can look like. How it would feel. I can educate myself, find what is mine to do, and get actively involved. I'm best able to do that when I've created a life where my own needs are being met. When my bills are paid. And I'm sleeping well. When my emotional and physical well-being is vibrant. When I feel safe and loved. When I have people in my life who understand oddball me. When life and I are working together, rather than against each other. From that stable foundation, I can make a greater impact. Have a more pronounced effect. If you want to change the world, start where you are. Prove to yourself you can do, be, and have more. Then share that more with others who need it. I honestly do believe we can have societies where everyone is fed, clothed, housed, educated, safe, fulfilled, and free. It just needs more of us manifestors to help usher in a better world. I'm in. I hope you'll join me.

There is nothing exceptional about me, I can assure you. Students will sometimes say, "Sure, that's fine for you. Easy for you to say. You're a mystical, spiritual badass who lives this stuff. I have a full-time job and an elderly parent I'm caring for. I'm just a regular person. I'm not special." I remind them, they are all just as special or not special as I am. The Universe does not discriminate. In Its eyes, we are all equal. I wasn't born under a lucky star. And I can assure you, no sane person, upon hearing my life story, would ever trade places with me. I've had more struggle, heartache, and adversity than most. And all of those painful experiences fueled the growth that has brought me to this place. I'm deeply in love with my life. Here's what may set me apart: I work these principles and practices. Practices are designed to be just that, practiced. I take my life and happiness seriously. I don't settle for mediocre because I've learned I don't have to. And neither do you. I worked at this for long enough that I reached a time when I no longer had to. Most often, blessings flow into my life. And when I hit walls, I know how to heal them, so flow can be restored once again.

Like in cooking, follow the steps of the recipes that I've shared here. Track your efforts and the results. What paid off and what didn't? Which did you enjoy? Which ones would you never do again? Pay attention. To your thoughts and feelings. To your experiences. Mind your excuses. Heal the resistance. And work what works. Work it with wild abandon. Work it with joy. And rejoice in all the ever-flowing good that comes.

Acknowledgments

To Joel Fotinos, for once again giving me a chance to take what I teach and bring it out into the world in a bigger and most beautiful way. And much gratitude to the right hand of the operation, Gwen Hawkes, for always having the answers and serving with professionalism, savvy, and kindness. Thank you both for all the encouragement, support, and extended deadlines!

For all the metaphysical teachers throughout the years who reached me through books, lectures, classes, and workshops. You drew on both ancient and modern wisdom, merging it with your own, to advance this knowledge further. Not limited to Catherine Ponder, Debbie Ford, Deepak Chopra, Denise Linn, Emma Curtis Hopkins, Ernest Holmes, Florence Scovel Shinn, Gail Straub, Iyanla Vanzant, Marianne Williamson, Michelle Wadleigh, Neale Donald Walsch, Roxanne Louise Miller, Tama Kieves, Toni Hamilton, and Wayne Dyer.

To my family. Thank you for understanding when I disappear. Writers do that. It's what we need to do to get the work done. I apologize for my absences. For all the times I'm too busy. I'm going to make it up to you!

To all my friends, my family of choice, spread out across the globe, who tolerate my insecurities and applaud my bravery. You make my life zing in every way.

To the Creative Collective—Donniee Barnes, Mary Kay Carney, and Sylvia Taylor—for making me accountable, always responding to my blocks with compassion, and urging me forward exactly when I needed it. Could not have written this without you all!

For Veronique Ramsey, who jumped forward to create all the illustrations for my first book when she was juggling countless responsibilities and two teens while packing to leave the country. You always give me a safe place to land, make me laugh, and encourage me when I get stuck or scared. Thank you for being a most cherished sister-friend.

Resources

Visit www.manifestingbook.com for free resources to support your manifesting journey. Includes downloadable PDFs, meditation and affirmation audios, song lists, and much more.

Index

Higher Power, 18–19
Higher Self, 18
Hill, Napoleon, 55, 166
hobbies, 147–48
Holmes, Ernest, 20, 99
home, 147
household items, 75
hugging up, 151–52
hydration, 28

images
  representing what you're creating,
    127–28
  taking photos, 26
  vision boards, 139–40
infinity energy exercise, 116–17
inspired action and asking for signs,
    103–11
intuition, 110
  ignoring, 219
"It," 17–20

job, *see* career
Jobs, Steve, 72
journals
  doubt, 200–201
  feelings, 195
  gratitude, 138
  manifestation, 135–38
  time, 162
  what must I become, 215–18
Jung, Carl, 4, 139

Kent, Germany, 50
Kieves, Tama, 1
Kiyosaki, Robert, 59
Knost, I. R., 230

Lee, Bruce, 29
leisure time, ideal, steps for
    manifesting, 170–71
"letter to a friend" process,
    126–27
levels of manifestation, 155–58
lists for manifestations, 113–18
longing, 216–17

love
  celebrating, 184
  embracing all forms of, 184
  see also romantic relationships

Mahfouz, Naguib, 191
making room for the new, 71–76
manifestation
  as alchemy, 6–7
  choosing one area to work on at a
    time, 221–22
  exploring practices for, 222
  journal of, 135–38
  levels of, 155–58
  making part of everyday life, 223
  picking target for, 143–53
  putting everything together, 221–24
  reasons to try, 7–12
  setting aside time for, 222
  starting small with, 221
  support for, 222–23
  what to do if it's not working (yet),
    215–19
  what to do when the opposite of what
    you wanted happens, 211–13
Manifesting Alchemy Practices, 87–89
  acting as if (faking it till you make
    it), 125–28
  affirmations and scripting, 91–96
  dancing your dreams, 129–33
  inspired action and asking for signs,
    103–11
  lists for manifestations, 113–18
  manifestation journal and gratitude
    journal, 135–38
  minding the monkey mind, 119–23
  prayers and affirmative intentions,
    97–102
  vision boards, 139–40
Manifesting Alchemy Principles
  deservability and open receiving,
    61–67
  focusing on the good, 47–54, 223
  give what you want to receive, 69–70
  making room for the new, 71–76
  stop waiting, 55–60

About the Author

Alissa Cutter

KRIS FERRARO is an author, international energy coach, teacher, and sought-after speaker. Leaving a lengthy career as a social service counselor to guide others in the energy and metaphysical practices she had used to heal herself, Kris empowers others through the profound promise that everyone can move from surviving to thriving. She frequently speaks to diverse groups on how purpose, love, faith, and balanced energy are the ancient antidotes to modern stress caused by our current climate of constant uncertainty. A lifelong learner in the areas of personal growth, healing, and religious/spiritual history and education, Kris applies this knowledge in her own life, teachings, writings, and her professional coaching practice. She is the creator of Spiritual Freedom Techniques, a series of processes that combine spiritual practices and principles with energy balancing for supercharged transformation. As a former punk rocker, radio DJ, and performance artist, it was in healing her severe social anxiety that she was finally able to uncover her purpose and truly shine, without panic. In addition to writing and creating curriculum on transformation, and producing a cutting-edge newsletter with original photography, she writes and performs spoken-word poetry and is an accomplished sculptor. When not traveling she lives in Montclair, New Jersey, with her cats, Ling and the Baby Cheetah. Her first book, *Energy Healing: Simple and Effective Practices to Become*

Your Own Healer, was a #1 bestseller on Amazon. Her latest, *Manifesting: The Practical, Simple Guide to Creating the Life You Want,* distills ten years of her best metaphysical teachings.

Learn more about Kris's programs, books, and services at:

www.krisferraro.com

www.manifestingbook.com

Find Kris on social media:

Facebook Community Page: "Emotional Alchemy with Kris Ferraro"

www.facebook.com/befreetoflourish